THE FUTURE OF FUTURES

Introduction by Andy Hines — 1	**Present** — 10	**Future** — 25
Past — 2	The Scenarios Question by Andrew Curry — 11	Crowdsourced Futures by Noah Raford — 26
The History of Futures by Wendy Schultz — 3	A New Typology of Wildcards by Oliver Markley and John Petersen — 16	Integral Futures by Richard A. Slaughter — 28
Most Important Futures Works — 8	Africa Futures by Tanja Hitchert — 17	From Values To Time by Marcus Barber — 33
Founding the APF: A Personal History by Christian Crews — 9	The APF Student Recognition Program by Verne Wheelright — 19	From Design Fiction To Experiential Futures by Noah Raford — 35
	The Temporary City: Rethinking Urban Futures by Cindy Frewen Wuellner — 20	Anticipation: The Discipline Of Uncertainty by Riel Miller — 40
	Futurists and 'The Black Swan' by Andy Hines — 22	The Future Is A Verb Not A Noun by Tom P. Abeles — 45
	Visual History of Futures — 23	Afterword: The Future Of Futures by Andrew Curry — 47

INTRODUCTION

by Andy Hines

Andy Hines, a founding member of the APF, is now Lecturer and Executive-in-Residence at the University of Houston's futures program.

The APF emerged ten years ago from hallway and lounge conversations that complained of the absence of an organization devoted specifically to the needs of the growing ranks of professional futurists. Once it had used up its quota of complaining, a cadre of founding members decided, in 2001, that it was time to do something.

A gathering of three dozen futurists who seemed to be interested in the idea of organizing around the idea of professional networking was convened in Seattle. And thus emerged the APF.

The early years were about putting in place enough structure to keep it going. This included deciding on a governing structure and forming a Board. The listserv became an early 'glue' for our virtual organization and is still cited as a valuable benefit. From there, websites, newsletters, and annual gatherings -- the first being a scenario development workshop on the future of futures – and later, professional development.

In our third year, we reached 200 members; membership now is around the 300-mark. Although the organization was founded in the United States by a group of American futurists, around two-fifths of the membership is now non-American.

As the organization has stabilized, it has also developed. New elements have been added to the APF's program, such as the Student Recognition Awards and the selection of Most Important Futures Works, both represented in this volume. Another milestone has been the evolution of the APF's leadership from the founders to a new generation, who are putting their stamp on the APF. It has become a more networked organization, in both senses of the word, using social media to extend its reach and running last year a virtual event – the V-gathering – which followed the sun for 18 hours from Europe to the United States to Australia. And this book is only one of a number of tenth anniversary initiatives.

I suspect that some are surprised that APF has made it to its tenth birthday, and is on a secure footing. Sometimes I think we underestimate our impact – I'm always struck by how students speak almost reverentially about the organization, and I think it's important to them, and the potential futurists alongside and behind them, that we exist. We're on the map, we have good relations with other organizations in the foresight ecosystem, and I think we can play an important role in supporting professional futurists and building the profession.

It is now fifty years since Herman Kahn first revealed his scenarios for 'thinking the unthinkable.' As the articles in this book suggest, all contributed by APF members, futures work seems on the edge of a profound transition. Professional practice will evolve as a result. The Association of Professional Futurists looks forward to playing its part as futures – as a practice and a discipline – moves into this next, exciting, phase.

PAST

'THE FUTURE IS CERTAIN. IT IS ONLY THE PAST THAT IS UNPREDICTABLE' – SOVIET-ERA RUSSIAN JOKE

THE HISTORY OF FUTURES

by Wendy Schultz

Wendy Schultz studied futures at the Hawai'i Research Center for Futures Studies, taught futures at the University of Houston-Clear Lake, and facilitates futures wherever she can from her base in Oxford, England.

Stars! Goats! Charred bones! Dice! God's breath! Enlightenment! Rationality! Calculus! Metahistorical patterns! Behavioralism! Insight! Multivariate analysis! Econometrics! Systems modeling! Scenarios! Big data! Machines of loving grace...

Extending our reach

What will Europe look like in 2025? or Hong Kong? Who will win the play-offs? Will the hurricane season be bad this year? How will the stock market perform next quarter? Will I acquire fortune and glory? Is the Apocalypse imminent?

Looking beyond the immediate energizes human nature. Our innate curiosity drives us to learn, explore, experiment, and seek to predict. In the words of Eleonora Masini: "People become human the moment they think about the future, the moment they try to plan for the future."

Where to start? Let's take a short ride in a very fast machine: 10,000 years of futures in 200 words. For thousands of years the shamans, mystics, priests, and oracles controlled the future -- or at least the production of images of it. This remained true up until the latter half of the twentieth century: the oracle at Delphi was replaced with the the Delphi method, but the images were still produced by academic elites for political and economic elites. Methods of reading the future in tea, entrails, or the i-Ching were simply replaced with slightly tidier techniques, although the notion that any technique was 'predictive' with regard to human systems went up with the turbulent smoke of chaos and complexity. Ambient informatics in the twenty-first century have started to decentralize the power core of futures thinking, while crowd-sourcing and multi-player games enrol more people in futures exploration.

Five ages of futures

That's still something of a blur. Let's slow down the machine and zoom in closer to pick out the brighter lights. There seems, at this height, to be five waves of futures work. The first wave, alluded to above, is the oral wave of the shamans and mystics, still embedded in the deep myths of futures practice; not just in the Delphi method, but in the 'Oracle' question of the Seven Questions method and the ubiquity of the 'Cassandra' problem in futures: even when you are convinced of a future outcome, it is difficult to persuade others to act on it.

Moving on we start to see a written wave, much of it outside of Europe. Some of these were early macrohistorians, such as Sīmǎ Qiān (around the second century BCE) and Ibn Khaldun (14th century), looking for patterns in the past and for cycles of repetition. Qiān, for example, charted virtue cycles in 30, 100, 300, and 1000-year spans. Ibn Khaldun traced patterns of nomadic conquest, consolidation, waste and decadence, and conquest. Their work and methods prefigured the work of later macrohistorians, such as Spengler, Hegel, Teilhard de Chardin, Toynbee and Sarkar.

If Nostradamus and his *Propheties*, in the 16th century, seem like a throwback to the days of the mystics, the English writer Thomas More and the Anglo-Irish scientist Robert Boyle prefigure important approaches to the future. In *Utopia* (1516), More sketched an image of the future as an aspiration, creating an enduring metaphor for an ideal society, an idea which recurs throughout the history of futures. Robert Boyle, a century later, wrote a 'wishlist for the future of science', which

– long before the science itself was feasible – mapped ideas for future researchers.

ENLIGHTENMENT AND PROGRESS

The third wave of futures studies is deeply embedded in the idea of progress through science, technology and rationalism. Voices such as de Condorcet and Auguste Comte emerge into view. But that story of progress encourages the development and the acceleration of resource extractive economies, and the development of a recurring argument in the history of futures between images of technology and images of the environment. The late 19th century sees competing narratives emerging from proto-science fiction. Jules Verne's *20,000 Leagues Under the Sea*, published in 1870, offered a positive image of an ecological future wrapped in a science fiction adventure. In *News From Nowhere*, in 1890, William Morris painted a future of human technology, pleasure in craft and creative work, and common property. The scientific romances of H.G. Wells included the millennia-spanning *The Time Machine*, published in 1895.

These early efforts in writing possible futures were followed by futures depicted in moving images. Both Verne and Wells inspired the first science fiction film, Georges Méliès 1902 *A Trip to the Moon*. In a more serious vein, Fritz Lang's 1927 *Metropolis* critiqued class divisions and introduced the first of many evil cinema robots. It was perhaps inevitable that technological innovation and space exploration emerged as strong themes in early 20th century thought about the future.

The influence of H. G. Wells – as writer and intellectual – on the development of futures can't be over-estimated. In 1902 he lectured at London's Royal Institution on "The discovery of the future"; 30 years later his talk on BBC Radio 4 was titled, "Wanted: Professors of Foresight".

By this time, we had seen the beginning of large scale national projects. In 1928, the USSR's first five-year plan was published by Strumlin et al; in the US, Herbert Hoover appointed the Research Committee on Social Trends, led by sociologist William F. Ogburn, to study social change across American society. It released the landmark report *Recent Social Trends in the United States* in 1933.

SYSTEMS, INTERCONNECTIONS, INTERDEPENDENCIES

The Great Depression and the experience of the Second World War perhaps represented the limits of the enlightenment project. But total war, in particular, accelerated experiments in technical forecasting and systems operations. A significant center for this in the US was the think-tank known as RAND. But all the countries embroiled in the war needed grand scale planning and forecasting both to mobilize the millions of men and women involved, and to provide the resources

Most Important Futures Works

Wendell Bell's **Foundations of Futures Studies** is the definitive introduction to the field from one of its most experienced practitioners. Foundations appears in two volumes. The first volume is a comprehensive description of the field – its history, purpose, principles, epistemology and methods. The second volume is less well-known. It is an argument for the existence of universal values and an appeal to futurists to promote those values in their work. – **Peter Bishop**

needed for their support. Systems science evolved side by side with futures studies during the 20th century. A 'sister science,' ecology, also emerged hand-in-hand with systems thinking. This is the fourth wave. The mid-1950s sees a series of seminal moments in the evolution of futures studies that give it shape for two generations.

In 1954, the International Society for the Systems Sciences (ISSS) was organized at Stanford University by Ludwig von Bertalanffy, Kenneth Boulding, Ralph Gerard, and Anatol Rapoport. Kenneth Boulding's work bridged systems science and futures studies, as seen in books such as *Evolution, Order and Complexity* and *The Future: Images and Processes*. A year later, Fred Polak's seminal work, *The Image of the Future* (1955), mirrored the early macrohistorians in tracing the rise and fall of civilizations and cultures, but created a foundational futures insight by linking civilizations' success to their core images of the future. This inscribed the notion of social vision in futures practice. In the wake of World War II, European scholars in particular were both revisiting the meaning of the good society and redesigning and rebuilding their shattered infrastructure. The vibrant school of futures thought that subsequently emerged in Europe also owes much to French philosopher and planner Gaston Berger, who coined the term *prospective* – the study of possible futures. Another French scholar, Bertrand de Jouvenel, founded the Association Internationale Futuribles in 1960 (the first futures organization), and captured both the need for, and the approach to, emerging futures thinking in 1961's *The Art of Conjecture*.

RAND continued the American tradition of technocratic forecasting it began in operations and weapons research for WWII through the '50s and '60s, and contributed to the development of futures methods such as Delphi surveys (Olaf and Helmer). Herman Kahn's work at RAND in 'thinking the unthinkable' about thermonuclear war was one of the first policy uses of scenario thinking. Meanwhile at Stanford Research International, similar technocratic approaches led to Russell Rhyne's explorations in melding field anomaly relaxation with morphological analysis, which gave rise to robust methodologies in multivariate scenario building. These were later picked up and expanded by Michel Godet in France and Tom Ritchey in Sweden.

FUTURES INSTITUTIONS

By the end of the 1960s futures thinking was beginning to be codified and its activities organized formally – first in professional conferences, assemblies, and organizations, and later as accredited academic programs. American publisher Ed Cornish and colleagues founded The World Future Society (WFS) in Washington DC in 1966; the World Futures Studies Federation (WFSF) had roots in the Mankind 2000 conference held in Oslo in 1967, although it was not founded until 1973. The first academic centers of futures thinking and research included the Vatican's Gregorian University; the Turku School of Economics in Finland; in Hungary at the Corvinus University of Budapest; the University of Houston-Clear Lake in Texas; and the University of Hawai'i's Research Center for Futures Studies. At these different institutions scholars such as Eleonora Barbieri Masini, Pentti Malaska, Erzsébet Nováky, Oliver Markley, Peter Bishop, and James Dator started to build the academic base of futures studies.

The **Five Waves** of **Futures**

Oral Tradition
For example: Shamans, mystics, priests and others

First Wave

Early Written Age
For example: Sīmǎ Qiān, Ibn Khaldun, Nostradamus, Thomas More, Robert Boyle

Second Wave

New stories

The combination of generational challenge, emerging environmental sciences, and oil shock changed the tone of futures work as it moved into the 1970s. One of the most ambitious futures projects – and one which has been influential for the past 40 years – was *The Limits to Growth* (1972) written by Dennis and Donella Meadows, Jørgen Randers and William Behrens, working with Jay Forrester at MIT, using systems dynamics to model the *global problematique*.

Limits, commissioned by the Club of Rome, heralded the addition of ecological and environmental themes in futures work to those of technology, space, and economic dynamism. Argentinean scholar Carlos Mallman critiqued *Limits'* assumptions via the Bariloche Model, highlighting the issues of developmental inequity between North and South embedded within the *global problematique*. A more common critique came from Herman Kahn, whose Hudson Institute championed technological optimism, for example in depicting a 200-year transition to global wealth. This often put him at loggerheads in public debates with the Meadows and their message of likely system collapse.

The oil shock also lent credibility to Shell's rich use of corporate and management futures work. In the 1970s, Ted Newland, Pierre Wack, Arie de Geus, and an ever-expanding series of colleagues created a global reputation for creative thinking about strategic possibilities via stories depicting alternative futures. Their work almost single-handedly sold the idea of scenario planning throughout the business world and across management schools.

In a more humanist vein, SRI's Willis Harman, Oliver Markley, and others gave impetus to another grand theme in futures. Harman and Markley published the landmark study on the future of human consciousness and evolution, *Changing Images of Man*, in 1982. Harman continued that work at the Institute of Noetic Sciences. Barbara Marx Hubbard's various books and activities at her Foundation for Conscious Evolution likewise extended this exploration of inner and spiritual frontiers.

One consequence of the expanding field was the development of textbooks specifically for futures studies graduate work. Jib Fowles' *Handbook of Futures Research* (1978) was the pioneer; Richard Slaughter's *Knowledge Base of Futures Studies* (1993) and Wendell Bell's *Foundations of Futures Studies* (1996) followed in due course.

Futures practice had globalized in tandem with the emergence of the new nations of the post-colonial world in the '50s and '60s. Leading thinkers considering long-range futures for the developing world included Ibrahim Abdel Rahman of Egypt; Mahdi Elmandjra of Morocco; Uvais Ahamed of Sri Lanka; Ziauddin Sardar of Pakistan; and Ashis Nandy of India – among many others. In 1996, after a three-year feasibility study hosted by the United Nations University, the Millennium Project was founded to formalize global participatory futures in a research think tank embracing an international network of futurists, scholars, business planners, and policy-makers. Its work continues today.

Another sign of a maturing field was the formation in 2002 of the newest international futures organization, the Association of Professional Futurists (APF), to promote futures practice (as Christian Crews relates elsewhere in this book).

Limits to Growth is one of the APF's Most Important Futures Works: see panel on page 27.

Extraction and enlightenment
For example: de Condorcet, Comte, H.G. Wells, Jules Verne, William F. Ogburn, Soviet planning

Third Wave

Systems and cybernetics
For example: RAND, SRI, *la prospective*, Herman Kahn, Shell, GBN, The Limits to Growth

Fourth Wave

Complexity and emergence
For example: Integral Futures, Causal Layered Analysis, experiential futures, anticipatory systems

Fifth Wave

 APF 2012. Some Rights Reserved.

Twenty-first Century – new frontiers

As futures studies and futures practice moves into the 21st century, it has started to undergo a sea change from the more technocratic and determinist theories and approaches which had served it since the 1950s. We are at the early stages of a fifth wave.

Connections between futures studies and psychological evolutionary theories, such as those of Clare W. Graves, added depth to the thread of exploring the futures of humanity's inner spaces. So too did the melding of futures theory and philosophy with integral philosophy. 'Integral Futures' – explored in a later essay – was initially championed by Slaughter, Voros, and other futures colleagues in Australia, and has since spread through the global futures community.

Other models have emerged in the early twenty-first century that also dig into the social and cultural substructures of changing human systems. Inayatullah's 'structuralism as method' – Causal Layered Analysis – and Lum and Bowman's Verge, which draws on ethnographic futures concepts, are two examples, both from alumni of the Hawai'i Reseach Center for Futures Studies.

The 'Pacific Shift,' as experienced by futures studies, is not only a shift towards deeper understanding of the hidden social and cultural determinants of our futures, but also a shift from the formalization of futures thinking in Europe and the USA to vibrant communities of futures practice throughout the Pacific Basin and Asia. The move in 1993 of the World Futures Studies Secretariat to Australia was an indicator of this. The futures program at Tamkang University in Taiwan and its *Journal of Futures Studies*, the explosive growth of interest in futures practice in Singapore and South Korea, in India and Thailand and Pakistan, all indicate the current extent of that shift.

Digital worlds, open sources, social networks

In the late twentieth century, systems thinking developments in the form of chaos and complexity theories enhanced understanding of the dynamics of intertwined human and planetary systems. These theories provided a paradigm of change as an emergent property of complex, adaptive living systems, explorable but rarely predictable.

Looking for seeds of the future visible in the present, we can see a clear and welcome trend towards decentralized, massively distributed and inclusive futures work. Global computing and interconnected communication support digital exploration of our possible futures with new levels of creativity, rigor, and participation. Ubiquitous sensor nets, massive data output, and the computing capacity to analyze it mean far greater granularity in our analysis of complexity, change and emergence. Immersive and programmable graphic environments such as Second Life allow people to experiment with realities they might want to create; global games such as *SuperStruct* and *Evoke*, developed by Jane McGonigal, engage participants from many cultures in devising solutions to future challenges and suggesting present action; designers are working with inventors, futures researchers, and community organizers to create experiential futures to incite exploratory conversations.

The futures are now for everyone to envision.

Note to readers: for reasons of space much has had to be elided or omitted; no disrespect or slight is intended to any idea, event, thinker, or organization. For an extensive, growing, collaborative view of the history of futures thinking, please see the 'history of futures thinking timeline' evolving online at Prezi.com.

Further reading

Bell, Wendell (1997), *Foundations of Futures Studies: Human Science for a New Era*, vol. 1 History, Purposes, and Knowledge. Transaction Publishers.

Kleiner, Art (1988), *The Age of Heretics: Heroes, Outlaws, and the Forerunners of Corporate Change*. Doubleday Business; 1st edition.

Masini, Eleonora (1982), "Reconceptualizing Futures: A Need and a Hope," *World Future Society Bulletin, Vol. 16(6)*.

Slaughter, Richard (ed.), *Futures*, Volume 37, Issue 5, Pages 349-444 (June 2005), Special edition on the World Futures Studies Federation.

Most Important Futures Works

The APF's Most Important Works program was founded in 2007 to call attention to works which have had a significant impact on the development of futures studies, and the first awards were made in 2008.

For the inaugural selection, only published books were eligible. Fifty-seven books were nominated, and the top ten were recognized by the APF.

A second round of awards was made in 2009, and eligibility was expanded to include digital works.

The third round of Most Important Futures Works is currently being judged, and will be announced later in 2012. There are short summaries throughout this book of some of the titles which have been honored or commended.

2008 Awards

The Art of the Long View (1991) by Peter Schwartz

Foundations of Futures Studies: Human Science for a New Era, vols 1 & 2 (1997) by Wendell Bell

The Knowledge Base of Futures Studies, vols 1-4, CD-ROM (2005) by Richard Slaughter (ed)

Limits to Growth (1972) by Donella Meadows, Dennis Meadows, Jørgen Randers, and William Behrens

The State of the World (annual series) by Worldwatch Institute

The State of the Future (annual series) by Jerome Glenn and Ted Gordon, Millennium Project

L'Art de la Conjecture (The Art of Conjecture) (1964) by Bertrand de Jouvenel

Futures Research Methodology Version 2.0 (2003) by Jerome Glenn and Theodore Gordon (eds), Millennium Project

The Age of Spiritual Machines (1999) by Ray Kurzweil

Collapse: How Societies Choose to Fail or Succeed (2005) by Jared Diamond

2009 Awards

Honors awards, 2009

SuperStruct by IFTF/Jane McGonigal, Jamais Cascio and Kathi Vian (2008), an online, multi-player game environment involving five critical global issues for the next decade

Integral Futures, Special Issue of *Futures* (Mar 2008), edited by Richard Slaughter, Peter Hayward and Joseph Voros

"Six Pillars: Futures Thinking for Transforming," in *Foresight* (2008) by Sohail Inayatullah

Honorable mentions

Six Degrees: Our Future on a Hotter Planet (2008) by Mark Lynas

Future Savvy: Identifying Trends to Make Better Decisions, Manage Uncertainty, and Profit from Change (2008) by Adam Gordon

Born Digital: Understanding the First Generation of Digital (2008) by John Palfrey and Urs Gasser

FOUNDING THE APF: A PERSONAL HISTORY

by Christian Crews

Christian Crews is the principal of AndSpace Consulting, where he applies foresight and design thinking to help companies innovate and grow. He has previously worked at Pitney Bowes, Waitt Family Foundation & Waitt Institute, and Toshiba International.

Each of the members of the APF has their own journey to it. For me the APF started in 2002. I was sitting on a shag carpet, surrounded by weird pillows and lava lamps, listening to the 30 attendees of the Applied Futures Summit tell how they became futurists.

The Summit was a single event organized by Michele Bowman, Richard Lum, Sandra Burchsted, Andy Hines, and myself, to bring experienced foresight professionals together to talk about the craft. It was held at the Future at Work exhibit in Seattle, a collaboration of designers, workplace anthropologists, and manufacturers who explored different ways people would be working in the future. During the storytelling, I was struck that we had similar paths into the field, yet diversity of experience and approaches. After the stories ended, I sensed something else beginning. A desire in the room to ensure this kind of magic would happen again, and that more could benefit.

I had been a part of previous discussions. Most of us had. For the graduates of the University of Houston-Clear Lake program in the room, we had gone from the high futurist-per square inch of the classrooms to serving as lone futurists in operationally focused organizations.

We had resorted to holding unofficial meetings at other conferences, some requiring jumping pool fences and dodging security guard flashlights. Some of us returned annually to UHCL for alumni gatherings. In most of these different sessions, the topic of a professional association came up.

We were frustrated by the way futures was perceived, and by the poor opportunities for professional development.

There is a basic need for those in any field to meet and talk, and to see the recognition in another's eyes validating your own experience. I helped organize the Summit to see if an annual event would feed that need – a trip to an interesting location every year to boost my methods and revitalize my passion for foresight. The Applied Futures Summit made it clear that need existed beyond Houston alumni.

At the Summit – attended by futurists educated at Houston and Hawai'i, those trained within corporations and consultancies, and some self-taught pioneers – we found we shared other concerns as well. Many were frustrated by the way the field was perceived, and by the limited ability to continue our professional development. Before the Summit these issues were seen as chronic problems. After the Summit, it seemed suddenly possible to address some of those long-time issues. I realized that a full professional association was worth the effort.

At the first APF Annual Gathering, held later that year in Austin, Texas, these hopes were affirmed. We discussed the future of the field, and learned how others use common tools. I got a lead that eventually led to my next job as a futurist. These qualities – enabling conversations about the field, learning and applying new methods, and professional development – were present from the beginning of the APF. They continue to be the bedrock of what makes it so important today

A more formal account of the APF's history, written by Andy Hines, can be found on its website at http://www.profuturists.org/history.

PRESENT

'I ASKED MYSELF ABOUT THE PRESENT: HOW WIDE IT WAS, HOW DEEP IT WAS, HOW MUCH WAS MINE TO KEEP' – KURT VONNEGUT

THE SCENARIOS QUESTION

by Andrew Curry

Andrew Curry, the editor of this book, has led scores of scenarios projects using a range of different approaches, and has written about scenarios methods.

Scenarios work is one of the distinctive practices of futures. In the minds of many it is associated strongly with the 2x2 'double uncertainty' matrix, in which 'important' future uncertainties are compressed into two significant themes of uncertainty, and a set of scenarios developed by exploring the worlds which emerge by combining the different outcomes.

However, this method wasn't always a dominant model, and it is worth exploring how it came to be so. Futures work is a relatively young discipline, and hasn't yet developed its equivalent of historiography, the branch of history which looks at why particular views of history attained prominence at particular times. In this essay, I am going to take a look at the history of scenarios practice through the lens of a nascent 'futurography' to understand the evolution of different scenarios practice at different times.

A Multiplicity of Methods

Scenarios can be defined as a group of stories which together describe a range of possible and coherent future worlds for a given domain or system. There is no shortage of scenario building methods. In our article, "Roads Less Travelled," Wendy Schultz and I explored four: the double uncertainty method, popularized by Peter Schwartz' book, *The Art of the Long View*; two methods used by the University of Hawai'i futures school, Futures Archetypes and Manoa; and Causal Layered Analysis, invented by Sohail Inayatullah, himself a Hawai'i alumnus. And beyond these, the list stretches down the hall. The French *prospective* school has its own scenario development techniques, and Morphological Scenarios (also known as Field Anomaly Relaxation, or FAR) have a long history. 'Pathway' scenarios methods have been widely used; 'trilemma' models exist; and there are scenario development methods based on soft systems modeling. Several of these are documented in the Millennium Project's *Futures Research Methods 3.0*. Even this list is far from complete. Close to two dozen methods are listed in the 2007 paper, "The Current State of Scenarios Methods," by Peter Bishop, Andy Hines, and Terry Collins, although some of those listed are visioning techniques. Philip van Notten has covered similar ground (with colleagues), as has Dennis List. Different methods have their strengths and weaknesses. The point is, as Wendell Bell observes, that "scenarios can be produced by any and all of the specific methods used by futurists."

The Art of the Long View

This leaves us still with the question of why, when there are so many ways of producing scenarios, the double uncertainty method has become so dominant. The answer seems to lie in a moment of publishing history. Peter Schwartz, who had run the Shell scenarios team through much of the 1980s and had left to set up the futures consultancy Global Business Network in 1987, published his book *The Art of the Long View* in 1991. The book itself is more about approach than method, and several of the scenarios projects described in it use other techniques, rather than the 2x2 double uncertainty method. However, as I understand the publishing history, the 2x2 method was codified and added as an appendix by his GBN colleague Jay Ogilvy. The method has a number of virtues, principally that it appears straightforward and produces a clear visual representation of a range of futures. It is, of course, also highly dependent on the quality of the initial framing question, and of the analysis that takes the work from the scanning stage to the identification of the matrix axes.

At the time, futures work was in something of a lull. The long boom of the '80s, and the end of the Cold War, meant that people were less anxious about the future than they had been. Schwartz, who was (and is) dynamic, charismatic, and well-connected, constructed GBN in a way that was bound to create attention. He was based in California – associated in the 1990s with the emerging digital wave; he attracted associates such as Stewart Brand and Brian Eno who were famous in their own right, and conveyed the strong message that GBN was not just another business futures house; and he developed a relationship with *Wired*, the house magazine of Silicon Valley, which in the '90s was one of the hottest publishing properties in the world. Schwartz's timing was also impeccable, for Pierre Wack's now famous articles in the *Harvard Business Review* in the mid-1980s had rekindled corporate interest in scenarios methods.

None of this should be taken as a criticism. At a time when futures work had lost its way, GBN reinvigorated it. His book, when it came out, was immediately influential (it is one of the APF's Most Important Futures Works: see panel). It showed that futures had a commercial and social value even in times of relative prosperity.

The 2x2 method is sometimes described as 'the Shell approach', with the halo this implies from

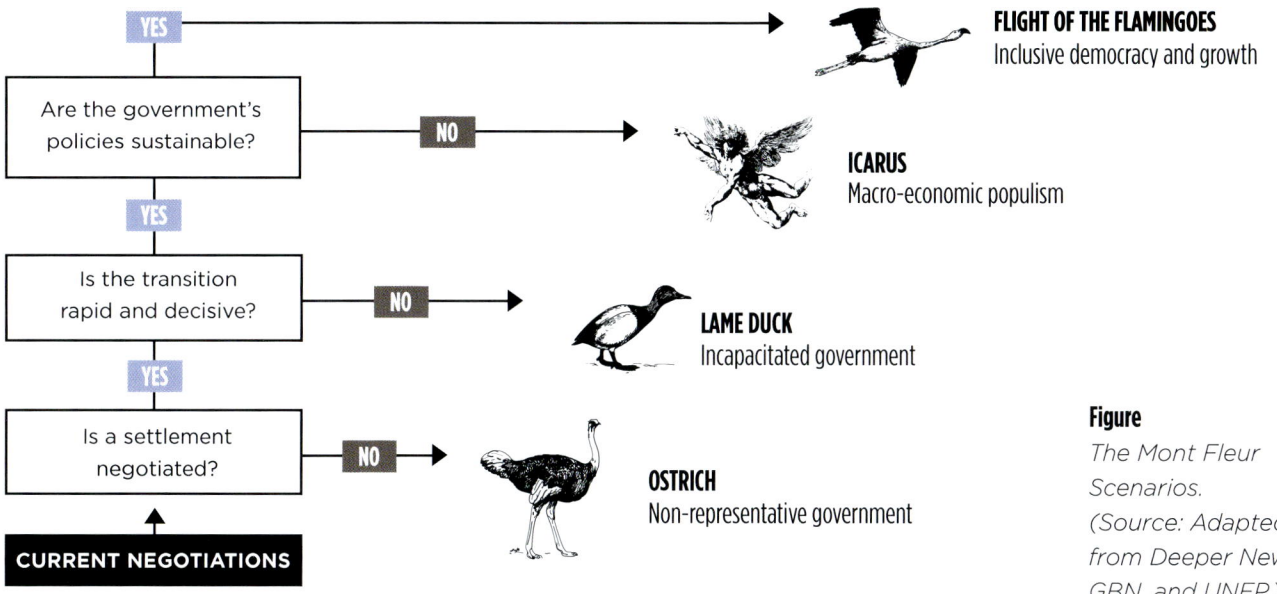

Figure
The Mont Fleur Scenarios. (Source: Adapted from Deeper News, GBN, and UNEP.)

Shell's use of scenarios to ride, so successfully, the 1970's oil price spike. In fact the method comes from SRI, another West Coast futures consultancy. Jay Ogilvy had joined GBN directly from SRI, and Schwartz had worked there before he went to Shell. There is an antecedent to the 'double uncertainty' model at SRI, in its 'scenario parameter matrix' associated with Tom Mandel, which produced four scenarios through a plot- or archetype-based framework covering optimistic, pessimistic, and present trends extended scenarios, together with one wildcard scenario. Shades of the parameter matrix can be seen in *The Art of the Long View*'s interest in 'plots' and stories.

For its part, Shell has been agnostic about methods. Pierre Wack's original oil price scenarios told their story through a set of pathways, as Art Kleiner explains in his counter-cultural business history, *The Age of Heretics*, and were developed partly through actor analysis and role-play.

The South African Mont Fleur scenarios, led by another Shell alumnus, Adam Kahane, were also built as a set of forking paths, as he explains in his book *Solving Tough Problems*. Similarly Shell has also used 'trilemmas', in which three sets of uncertainties are identified (even if such scenario sets are sometimes 2x2x2 'triple uncertainties' traveling lite), and sometimes just scenario pairs, even if such an approach is usually regarded as poor practice. Wack himself, though sometimes over-credited for the Shell scenarios work, evolved his practice towards an inductive approach based on deep 'seeing' and on the identification of the 'predetermined elements,' also discussed at some length in *The Art of the Long View*. Arguably the scenarios approaches described by Kees van der Heijden are closer to Shell's methods.

The Invention of Scenarios

Going further back into the history, Herman Kahn is generally regarded as the first person to use the word 'scenarios' to describe a range of possible futures, the inspiration having come from a screenwriting friend. Much of his research was funded by the military and – as is well-known – dealt with nuclear war. It was designed, in Kahn's famous phrase, to help people to 'think the unthinkable.' His method, largely undocumented, drew more on game theory and operations research, along with a dollop of 'genius forecasting', than techniques we would today associate closely with futures work. As Joseph Coates has observed, "There are no Kahnian disciples, there is no Kahnian school, there is no conceptual methodological framework he developed that others follow through with."

There is a wider story here. It wasn't just Kahn who had problems systematizing his methods. Roy Amara memorably described future work as being about preferred, possible, and probable futures, but it took practitioners some years to move from the 'genius' approaches of Kahn and other proto-futurists of the '60s (a group which can be thought of as including Alvin Toffler, John McHale, Daniel Bell, Lester Brown, Harrison Brown, and Roberto Vacca, among others) to build repeatable methods to develop the 'possible futures' of scenarios. Even within Shell, according to Art Kleiner's account, where Ted Newland and Pierre Wack enjoyed a sympathetic and well-funded environment, it took them three attempts over several years to develop a set of scenarios worth sharing more widely. The history of success, as ever, is built on a history of failures.

Looking at it through this lens, it is possible to believe that the success of the 2x2 method is because it took something difficult – the practice of scenario building – and simplified it in such a way that people were confident that

Most Important Futures Works

The Art of the Long View is perhaps the best introduction to the futures field for a person who asks, "So what do futurists do?" It comes from a well-known, authoritative source (Peter Schwartz). It articulates and demonstrates the use of the basic principles of the field, particularly the role of uncertainty in long-term futures requiring the use of scenarios rather than single-valued predictions. It is full of great stories and case studies, and it contains the steps for the famous GBN scenario development process in the Appendix. – **Peter Bishop**

they could apply it. But is also possible to think that something has been lost in this process. As Napier Collyns, a veteran of both Shell and GBN, put it in an interview in 2007: "In my experience, scenario planning is an interpretive practice – it's really closer to magic than technique. ... Look long enough, hard enough, and the pieces will fall into place. Magic is a very difficult thing – most people spend their whole life cutting magic out."

The various scenarios methods which have emerged in the 50 years since Herman Kahn reflect most of the interdisciplinary roots of futures. These come from three main sources: from cybernetics and systems, from sociology (through Emery and Trist, and separately, through visioning practitioners such as Elise Boulding), and from political science, notably represented through the contribution of the Manoa School at the University of Hawai'i. And as Roberto Poli has written recently, there was also a fourth source, that of philosophy, which became submerged in the 1960s but seems to be re-emerging now. (Pioneers here include Ossip Flechtheim, Gaston Berger, and Fred Polak).

A Spectrum of Methods

It is possible to characterise methods as running (crudely) on one spectrum – in terms of methods – from 'harder' more technically-oriented approaches to softer, more intuitive methods, and on another – in terms of frameworks – from frameworks which focus more on structure and those which focus more on values.

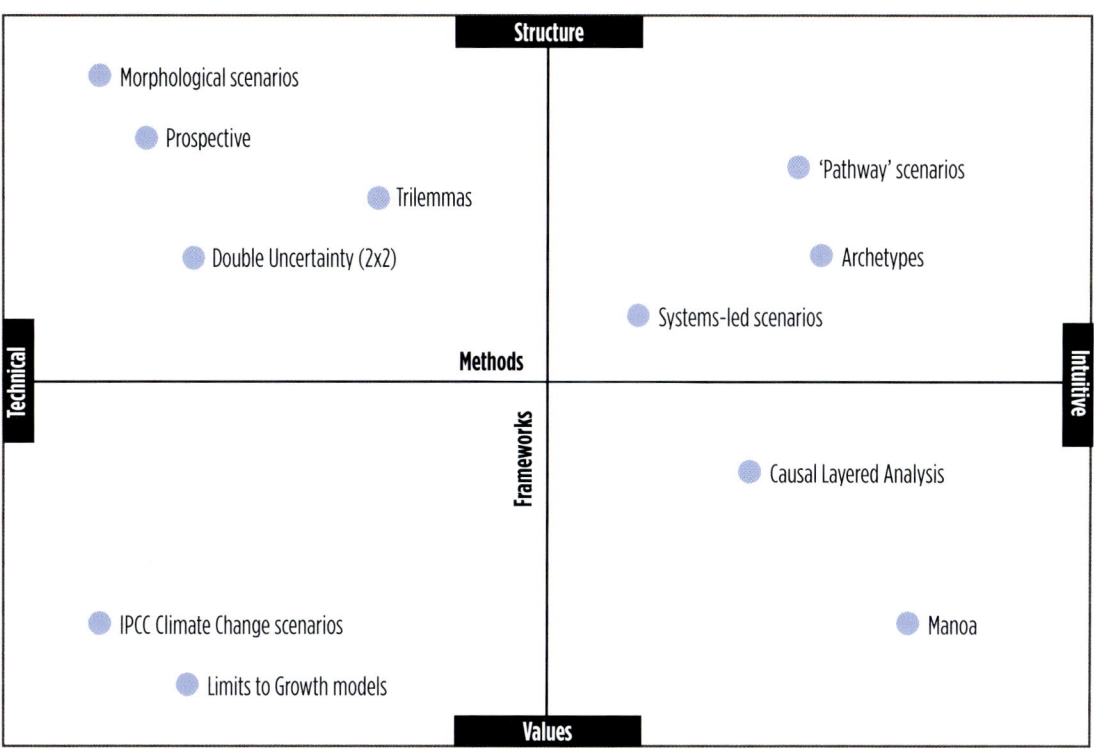

Figure
*Mapping scenarios techniques.
(Source: Andrew Curry)*

In very general terms, the more technical (and more structural) scenarios methods evolved first, perhaps reflecting the initial customers in government and business.

There is some correlation between harder and structural approaches, and more intuitive and more values-based approaches, but importantly also some approaches which sit in the other quadrants. Pathway scenarios, for example, are generally both structural and intuitive, while the IPCC scenarios are technically-oriented but clearly led by values.

A new method such as Causal Layered Analysis, which is intended as a broader approach to futures as a whole, but has a scenario building approach embedded within it, evolved at least in part to fill perceived gaps in existing methods. It draws on structural approaches, while being deeply underpinned by values, and tends to the intuitive rather than structural. The Three Horizons approach, originally devised by Bill Sharpe and Tony Hodgson, which I have helped to develop, can also be read as a way to bridge between structure and values.

From a 'futurography' perspective Richard Slaughter's critique of scenarios approaches which emphasize the empirical and external as objectifying existing power relationships, leading to what he called in *Futures Beyond Dystopia* a 'flatland' in which "current ideologies ... were insufficiently problematized and seen as natural" is part of this story too. Perhaps it is not coincidence that he was able to develop this critique at a distance, from the different cultural perspective afforded by Australia. Geography matters. And it is relevant that these methods emerged towards the end of the long global boom, at a time when the values which underpinned it were starting to be questioned.

As futures work continues to evolve, we will see new challenges to scenarios methods, and new methods developed. The jury is still out on whether, for example, scenarios will be able to absorb questions of complexity while remaining useful as 'futures objects' which are sufficiently straightforward to enable participants to have useful conversations about possible futures and consequent present actions. What we can be sure of, as the discipline matures, is that the process of selecting a method will become less prompted by habit and familiarity, and more by reflection. This is as it should be; it is a sign of a practice which is grown-up enough to ask itself questions. In the process, perhaps it will also rediscover some magic.

With thanks to Wendy Schultz and Napier Collyns for comments on earlier versions. Any errors are mine alone.

Further reading

Bell, Wendell (2009), *Foundations of Futures Studies*. Transaction Publishers (5th printing).

Bishop, Peter, Andy Hines and Terry Collins (2007), "The current state of scenario development: an overview of techniques," *Foresight*, Vol. 9(1).

Coyle, Geoffrey (2009), "Field Anomaly Relaxation (FAR)," *Futures Research Methods 3.0*. Millennium Project.

Curry, Andrew and Anthony Hodgson (2008), "Seeing in Multiple Horizons: Connecting Futures to Strategy," *Journal of Futures Studies*, Vol. 13(1).

Curry, Andrew and Wendy Schultz (2009), "Roads Less Travelled," *Journal of Futures Studies*, Vol. 13(4).

van der Heijden, Kees (1996), *Scenarios: The art of strategic conversation*. John Wiley and Son.

Inayatullah, Sohail (2004), *The Causal Layered Analysis Reader*. Tamkang University Press.

Jefferson, Michael (2012), "Shell scenarios: What really happened in the 1970s, and what may be learned for current world prospects," *Technological Forecasting and Social Change*, 79.

Kahane, Adam (2004), *Solving Tough Problems*. Berrett-Koehler.

Kleiner, Art (1996), *The Age of Heretics*. Nicholas Brealey Publishing.

List, Dennis (2005), *Scenario network mapping: The development of methodology for social inquiry (doctoral thesis)*. Division of Business Enterprise, University of South Australia.

van Notten, Philip, Jan Rotmans, Marjolein van Asselt, Dale Rothman (2003), "An updated scenario typology," *Futures*, 35.

Poli, Roberto (2011), "Steps Toward an Explicit Ontology of the Future," *Journal of Futures Studies,* Vol. 16(1).

Schwartz, Peter (1991), *The Art of the Long View*. Doubleday.

Sharpe, Bill and Kees van der Heijden (eds) (2007), *Scenarios for Success*. John Wiley and Son.

Slaughter, Richard (2004), *Futures Towards Dystopia*. RoutledgeFalmer.

Wack, Pierre, (1985), "Scenarios: uncharted waters ahead" and "Scenarios: shooting the rapids," *Harvard Business Review*, September-October and November-December.

A NEW TYPOLOGY OF WILDCARDS

by Oliver Markley and John Petersen

In long-range forecasting, futurists sometimes speak of 'wild cards' – usually defined as possible events that are considered to have a low probability of occurrence, but a very high impact (often negative) if they were to occur. An asteroid hitting the earth is sometimes used as a clear-cut example.

Although the following distinction has not yet appeared in the literature of futures research to my knowledge, I believe it is self-evidently useful to think of a second distinct type of wild card:

- Type I Wild Card: low-probability, high-impact, high-credibility
- Type II Wild Card: high-probability, high-impact, low-credibility

It is also useful to distinguish a Type III Wild Card, defined as being a Type II wild card that has come into enough public awareness as to engender heated dispute about its causal credibility (and derivatively, its assumed probability). Thus, the following additional typology of wild cards is proposed:

- Type III Wild Card: high probability, high-impact, disputed-credibility
- Type IV Legitimated Critical Forecast: high-probability, high-impact, high-credibility.

The lack of credibility that characterizes a Type II Wild Card can stem from at least four sources:

- **Ignorance** – where the relevant knowledge about the wild card has not yet disseminated
- **Disbelief** – where there is an active belief in the impossibility of the wild card
- **Disinformation** – where the relevant knowledge about the wild card has been camouflaged by propagandistic distortion
- **Taboo** – 'Elephants in the living room' that if you even talk publicly will severely undermine your legitimacy as a credible actor.

The whole Global Warming hypothesis is probably the most well-known contemporary example of what (for scientific thinkers at least), was originally a Type I Wild Card (i.e., there was general acceptance of the science involved, just no notion that the probability of high levels of atmospheric CO_2 was so great). It became a Type II Wild Card for politicians and others moved by industry-sponsored propaganda that

> The Global Warming hypothesis has moved from being a Type I Wild Card to Type IV - high probability, high impact, and high credibility.

discredited the science, then moved into the Type III phase as the debate heated up. Now, for most informed observers, it has attained the legitimacy of a credible, but 'wild' forecast (i.e., high probability, high impact, and high credibility).

This is a short extract from the Compass article. Longer journal articles exploring this can be found online at http://www.imaginalvisioning.com/anticipating-disruptive-surprises-with-futures-research/.

Compass, **Third Quarter, 2009.**

Oliver Markley is Professor Emeritus of Human Sciences and Studies of the Future, Univ. Houston-Clear Lake; John Petersen is Founder and President of The Arlington Institute.

AFRICA FUTURES

by Tanja Hichert

Tanja Hichert is a South African futures and foresight practitioner. She also serves as director of the South African Node of the Millennium Project, and is a research associate at Stellenbosch University's Institute for Futures Research.

Let me start by stating the obvious: Africa is not one country. It is a vast, complex continent consisting of 55 countries, home to just over a billion people speaking well over a thousand languages. Africa is the cradle of humankind. Together with its people, it is the most resilient place on earth. It is still there, intact as Africa and African, despite slavery, colonialism, decolonization, and being a pawn of competing power blocs during the Cold War.

Africa has experienced immense political transitions, and will continue to do so. The story of our time, though, is the unparalleled economic transition sweeping the continent. Whether this will ultimately lead to industrialization, modernity and high levels of human development is an open question. Africa's future is not a given; trying to extrapolate trends, make comparisons, or take an Afro-optimist vs. Afro-pessimist view quickly leads to intellectual frustration.

In this article I will sketch out some of the driving forces shaping Africa and their associated uncertainties, even while allowing that these are fraught with uncertainty and ambiguity, and that data are often unreliable and hard to come by.

A sampling of these forces include:

- Africa's population is currently just over 1 billion people. Projected trends indicate that this figure could double by 2036 and that half its population will be under the age of 20. Is this a demographic dividend, as was the case for East Asia, or a demographic disaster? It could be neither…

- Growing mid-size and mega cities, and their slums. Does this mean a movement of people out of rural areas and off the land, or high population growth rates in the cities? It could be both…

- Africa's strategic (geopolitical) importance should grow due to finite global natural resources and aging workforces in developed countries. But will it…?

- Comparatively strong economic growth driven by global resource and commodity demand. Will strong economic growth lead to modernity, industrialization and consumerism, or can Africa leapfrog this…?

- More mainstreaming of trade and development policies as well as some progress in the area of regional trade agreements to 'open up' potential consumer markets of emerging African economies.

- Continued and increasing investment in infrastructure to facilitate resource and commodity exports.

- Despite the progress made in addressing poverty, from a global perspective this will increasingly be an Africa-only problem.

- Human and economic development, but this will not necessarily lead to a marked improvement in governance. In many places corruption is a culture strengthened by company bribes, including those by international companies. Good governance requires the transformation of some entrenched habits and practices.

- Capital markets are not strong and the market capitalization of listed companies is low. Issues include the dominance of state-owned and state-controlled enterprises, when compared with weak business organizations. There are inadequate administrative systems and weak human resource institutions.

- A continued lag in the adoption of technological 'solutions' to the challenges of urbanization, environmental degradation and climate change coupled with increasing levels of ICT adoption and adaptation to the African milieu.

- Continued and increasing investment in agriculture, not necessarily to the benefit of Africa's poor, who are vulnerable and food insecure.

- Africa has, and will continue to have, the lowest life expectancy at birth, with many Southern African countries experiencing declining life expectancies due to HIV/AIDS.

- Extreme climate conditions – Africa will be the hardest hit.

These, and more, driving forces could lead anywhere and nowhere – because there is always something new out of Africa, yet some things in Africa never change, and often the best never happens, nor the worst. For those wanting to engage with Africa's future(s) it may be better (and more fun) instead to take a complexity approach and embrace the lack of certainty and knowledge that we so crave. To be resilient and responsive like an African knowing that anything or nothing can happen. To free ourselves of the preoccupation with the inherently unknowable, and rather direct energy towards action in the service of a hopeful, exciting, ethical, future that we can help to create.

THE **TRUE SIZE** OF **AFRICA** by **Kai Krause**

"A small contribution in the fight against rampant immappancy. Graphic layout for visualization only (some countries are cut and rotated). But the conclusions are very accurate."

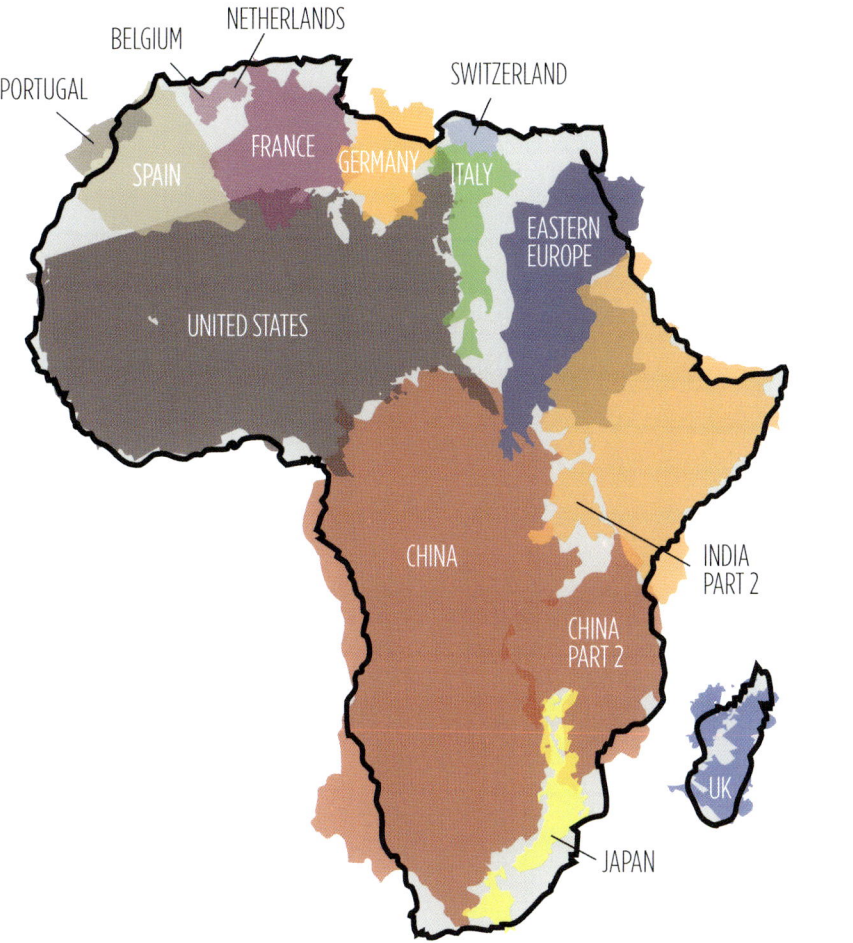

Map of Africa by Kai Krause. This is a Public Domain image published under a Creative Commons license.

Africa has a tiny but vibrant futures and foresight community that holds its own amongst the best in the world. Probably because it cuts its teeth in such a stirring, stimulating environment.

THE APF STUDENT RECOGNITION PROGRAM

by Verne Wheelwright

The APF launched its annual competition for graduate students in Foresight and Futures Studies in 2008, sending invitations out to 11 universities, based on research by Jose Ramos and a survey by John Smart. In 2012, this number will increase to 28 schools, from 22 different countries, as the number of schools offering Masters degrees in Foresight and Futures Studies continues to grow. There are three categories (Individual Masters student, Team (Masters) and Published Paper by a Ph.D. student). Three awards are offered in each category.

The winners in the first full three years also reflect the APF's international outlook. Inevitably, they include graduate student futurists from both the United States and Australia, but there have also been multiple winners from universities in each of Hungary, Finland and Mexico. One barrier in the early days of the competition was translation, since the APF did not have the resources to translate non-English papers. However, this is a problem which is being solved by technology; for the 2011 competition, currently being judged, machine translation has made huge strides, which has enabled the APF to welcome papers in many languages.

Subjects of winning papers have been diverse, and the methods used have been wide ranging. Just looking at the winners in 2010, they range from essays on the futures of literacy, mobile phones and multi-player games to postgraduate papers on the nature of futures knowledge.

Full details of the Student Recognition Program can be found on the APF website at www.profuturists.org. Please contact APF if you are involved in a futures Masters or Doctoral program and would like to be invited to take part.

Most Important Futures Works

Futures Research Methodologies is a CD-ROM-based resource edited by Jerome Glenn and Theodore Gordon. The approach is straightforward. Each method is described by a futurist or expert associated with it, and each essay runs through in turn the method's history, a description, how to apply it, its strengths and weaknesses, and areas of innovation. The 'Most Important Futures Works' accolade was awarded to Version 2.0. New material is added to each edition; version 3.0, released in 2010, covers more than 30 methods. It is an essential futures resource. – **Andrew Curry**

THE TEMPORARY CITY: RETHINKING URBAN FUTURES

by Cindy Frewen Wuellner

The image of the frontier is probably one of the oldest images of mankind [sic], and it is not surprising that we find it hard to get rid of. – Kenneth Boulding

During the last century, we saw cities expand rapidly, creating the first agglomerations of twenty million and now over thirty million people. Yet while China and India together are expected to add 100,000 people every day from now until 2025, some cities in the United States and nearly all in Europe are depopulating. As a further complication, the massive Asian urbanization may reverse itself in the next few decades, leaving vacant vast amounts of recently created real estate. The story of twenty-first century cities is more likely to be about undoing development than exploding growth.

In other words, like other types of market bubbles, peak urbanization is a real possibility. What do we decide to build today, knowing the next generation may be saddled with over-built cities? That question, and that perspective, should produce very different kinds of planning and construction decisions, yet few are talking about it. We have no useful models for the temporary city, and we struggle to re-imagine the shrinking city. As with the frontier, the urban imagination lives in a world of continual expansion. But what we need are models that allow for both changing populations and a conscious, and conscientious, urban legacy. It's possible that the next generations will value a light footprint above all else.

Simultaneously, tools for imagining the future are growing in both scale and capacity. Real-time big data, online social networks, and three-dimensional digital imagery are making urban futures increasingly rich and robust. Urban futures enable futurists and urban experts to develop more complete, articulated scenarios informed by social, environmental, and economic data. In turn, these more fully imagined scenarios shape our awareness of the possibilities. We can, in effect, experience the future before it arrives.

Collaborations between designers and futurists offer fertile territory. Descending from the detached helicopter perspective of the planner or the statistician, we can blend the aesthetic experience of the designer with the data-rich scenarios of futurists to construct lived-in futures. As technology advances, we will experience future cities laden with textures, smells, tastes, even movement through space. In fact, we might even say we will travel in time.

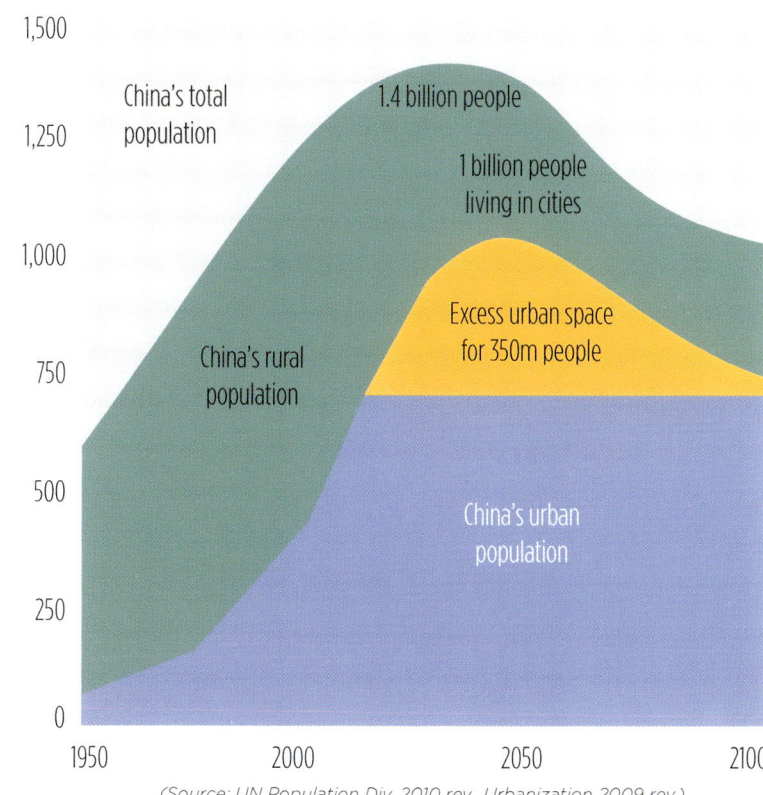

Figure *The rise and decline of urban China*

(Source: UN Population Div. 2010 rev., Urbanization 2009 rev.)

Dr Cindy Frewen Wuellner FAIA, architect and urban futurist, consults and writes about 21st century cities and teaches at the University of Houston futures program. She has designed courthouses, zoos, schools, barns, city halls, log cabins, police facilities, and a downtown civic commons. She chairs the APF board.
http://urbanverse.net

And we will not be alone. Awareness of alternative urban futures, once the domain of experts, is becoming more demotic and more democratic. Individuals, neighborhoods, corporations, non-profits, and governments will all have their own ideas. Using new information and tools to map the possibilities, we may shed the old models predicated on economic growth. We may, instead, learn how to 'unbuild' as well as build, adapting existing terrain instead of constantly seeking fresh territory. For that, we need new metaphors and models to see urban living with fresh eyes.

As an architect and futurist, it is a disappointment that cities have been largely responsible for the environmental crisis. We knew the basics of sustainability, but failed to persuade. Unusually, though, we have a second chance: a second chance to imagine cities that foster well-being, productivity, and resilience, whose social infrastructure is far stronger than concrete and steel.

The quote at the top of this essay is from "The Economics of the Coming Spaceship Earth", a presentation given by Kenneth Boulding in 1966.

Further Reading

Alexander, Christopher (1979), *The Timeless Way of Building*, Oxford Press, New York.

Brugmann, Jeb (2009), *Welcome to the Urban Revolution: How Cities are Changing the World*, Bloomsbury Press, New York.

Gehl, Jan (2010), *Cities for People*, Island Press, Washington, DC.

Hall, Peter and Kathy Pain (2009), *The Polycentric Metropolis: Learning from Mega-City Regions in Europe*, Routledge, London.

Jackson, Tim (2011), *Prosperity Without Growth, Sustainable Development Commission*, London.

Register, Richard (2006), *Ecocities: Rebuilding Cities in Balance with Nature*, Revised Edition, New Society Publishers, Gabriola Island, BC.

Rogers, Richard (1997), *Cities for a Small Planet*, Faber and Faber, London.

United Nations Human Settlement Programme (2011), *Cities and Climate Change*: Global Report on Human Settlements 2011. Earthscan, London.

COMPASS
by Jim Mathews

The APF's newsletter was first published in 2003, and contained news of developments in the APF along with some short pieces on topics of interest. In the intervening years, it has evolved into today's APF Compass, a quarterly softcopy publication which combines some of the functions of a traditional newsletter (such as updates from the Board and news from members) with articles of interest to the futurist community, such as book reviews and articles on methods.

There is a small selection of edited pieces from the Compass across the years in the rest of this book which gives a flavor of this content. (More are available on the public website). Members, meanwhile, have full access to the Compass archive in the members' section of the website.

FUTURISTS AND 'THE BLACK SWAN'

by Andy Hines

I wonder how many more bestsellers will be written about the future with no mention of foresight or futurists? Once again, I've somewhat reluctantly forced myself to look at another bestseller that clients are talking about and I can no longer avoid. I anticipate a familiar experience of some noted authority of some sort discovering and reporting on the future in a highly engaging and readable fashion – and ignoring our nascent field. The latest entry is Taleb's *The Black Swan*. I approach this work from the perspective of trying to crack the code. How does Taleb, in this case, package the need for the very basic tenets of foresight and climb the bestseller list with it. What are we futurists missing?

This book makes an excellent case for the formation of a field devoted to foresight. If we did not exist, it would be a welcome push to get to work (and maybe it does serve that purpose anyway). It includes 29 pages of references, yet not a single professional futurist is mentioned. You'd think, maybe just by accident, but no, not a single one – as far as I can see.

It is a work that pokes fun at forecasting, mostly economic forecasting. Not a single mention of 'scenarios.' The term does not appear in the index. No mention of wildcards! The core message of the book is that since we are so bad at forecasting, we should simply avoid it.

We are treated to several entertaining chapters on the foibles of forecasting that includes all the typical errors and biases. It's an interesting book. A great read, an elegant case for the need for foresight. Just that minor oversight of, well, futurists. So, beyond complaining, what is this telling us? Whether the oversight was intentional or not, it suggests that there is no penalty for doing so. I don't recall any mainstream book reviews that flogged him for ignoring foresight (though I wasn't paying much attention). So, we are still on the margins – not exactly news.

***Compass*, Fourth Quarter, 2011.**

Andy Hines, a founding member of the APF, is now Lecturer and Executive-in-Residence at the University of Houston's futures program.

Most Important Futures Works

I realized when I started working as a futurist that there was no shortage of predictions available to leaders and decision-makers looking to anticipate the future, but that they were of very mixed quality. I wrote **Future Savvy** to help people apply some futures quality control. Which forecasts should you take seriously, which should you be wary of, and which should you throw out entirely? So I included a battery of tests designed to reveal any forecast's strengths and weaknesses. And since hindsight is such a wonderful asset for a futurist, I also put my own judgment on the line – by assessing some predictions that had not yet reached their forecast date. – **Adam Gordon**

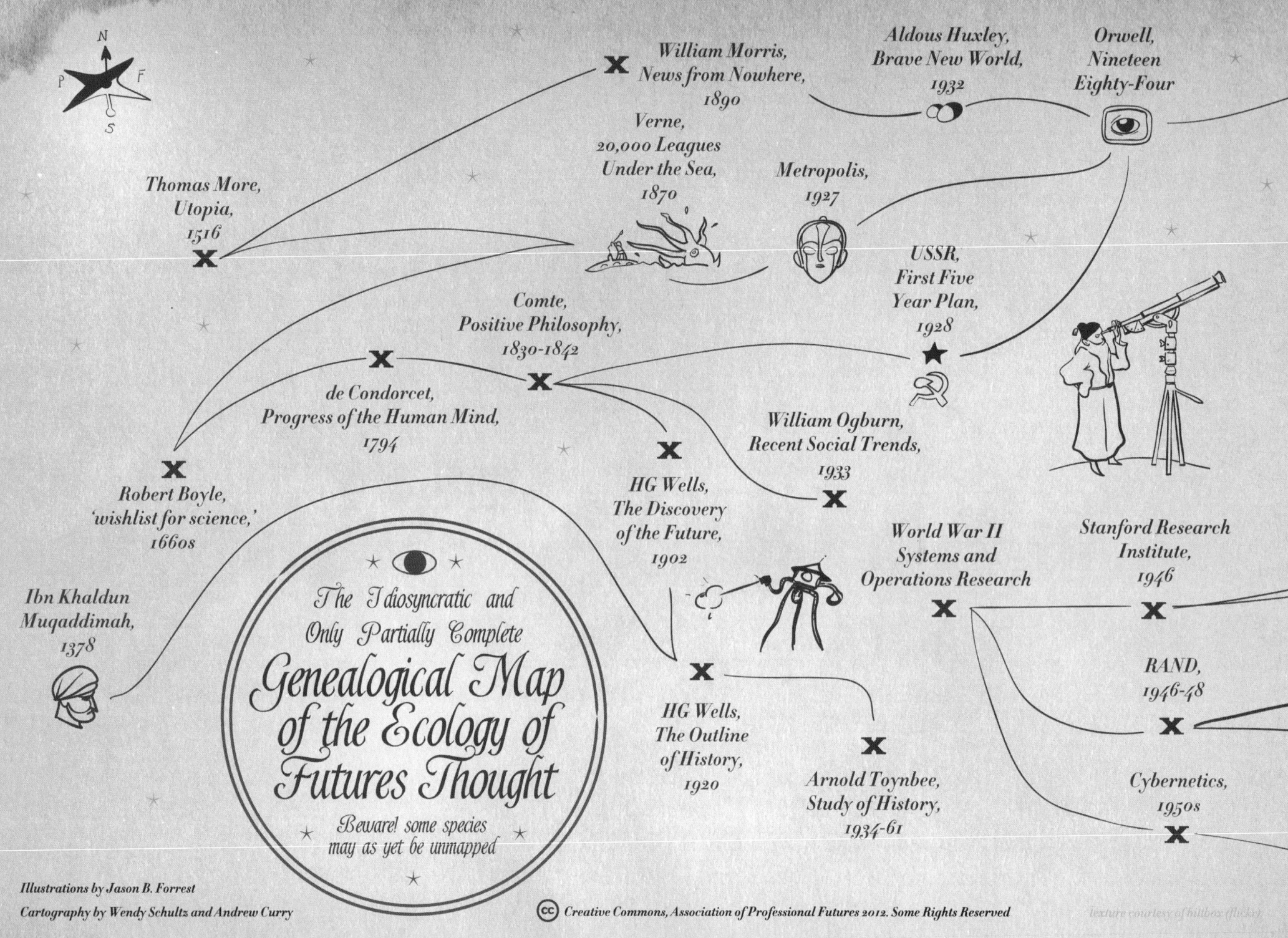

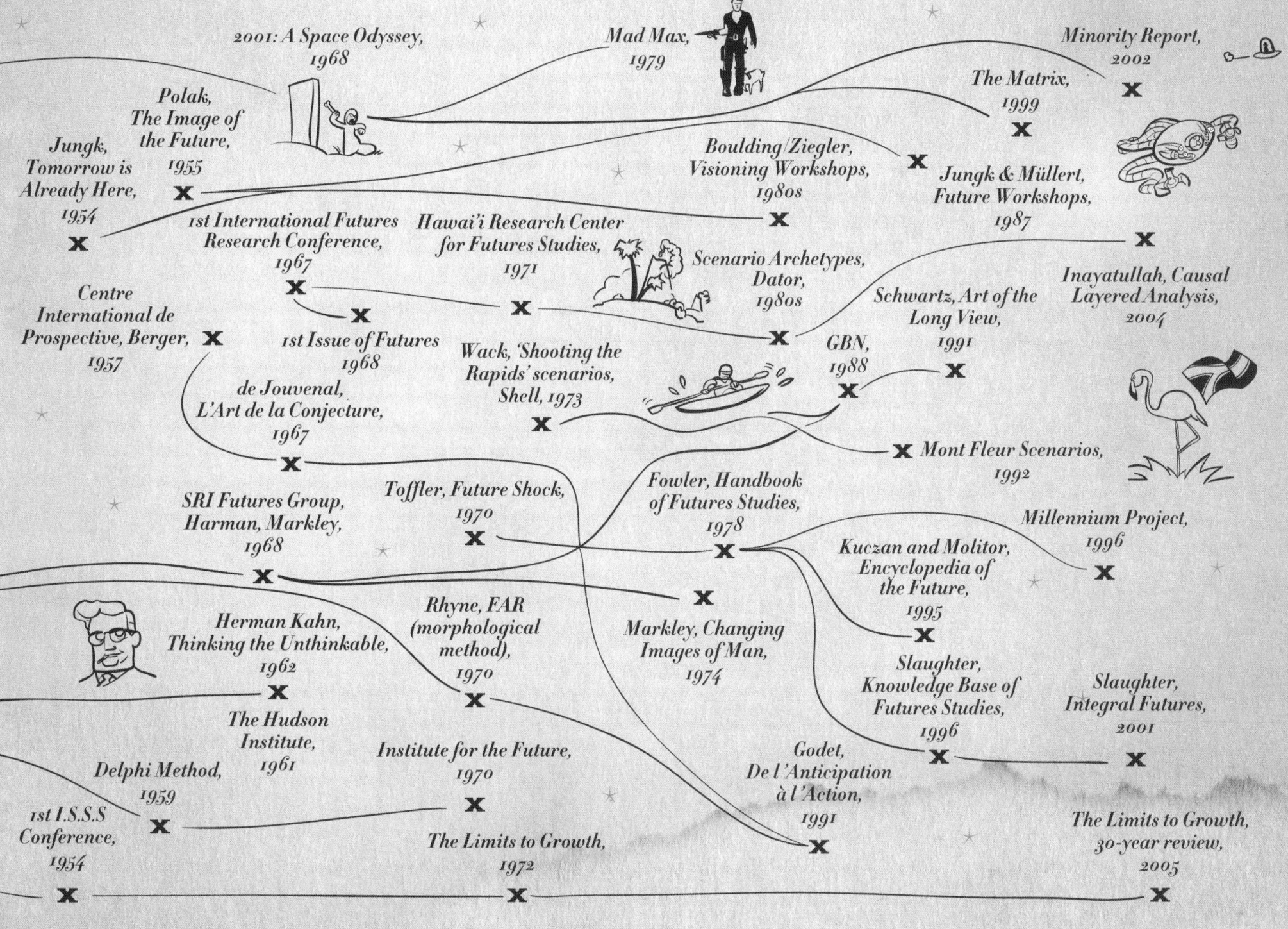

FUTURE

'THE FUTURE IS A VERY MURKY PLACE. THERE ARE NO EYEWITNESS ACCOUNTS, NO FIRST HAND EVIDENCE'
— W. WARREN WAGAR

CROWDSOURCED FUTURES

by Noah Raford

Jeff Howe defined crowdsourcing as, "the act of a company or institution taking a function once performed by employees and outsourcing it to an undefined (and generally large) network of people in the form of an open call." Under this definition, many parts of the futures process could be "outsourced to the crowd," at least in theory.

In practice, however, most crowdsourcing efforts related to futures and scenario work address only the earliest stages of the process, those related to environmental scanning and the collection of drivers. While there are exceptions, the bulk of futures' examples that have engaged crowdsourcing techniques focus on this early stage. There are excellent examples ranging from trend databases such as Shaping Tomorrow to weak signal databases such as TrendWiki. Many advertising and creative services agencies practice similar forms of environmental scanning as well, more commonly known as 'cool hunting.'

This kind of approach is an important one. Evidence suggests that the Web can enhance both the breadth and depth of our horizon scanning activities by, for example, providing 'always-on' monitoring and 'at your fingertips' evidence for almost any weak signal or emerging trend.

Pitfalls of Crowdsourcing

My own experience testing these approaches, however, suggests that the use of the Web in this way has several pitfalls. On the upside, crowdsourcing the 'drivers' process can provide an order of magnitude increase in speed, depth and breadth over a traditional scanning exercise. It also allows more people to be involved, over a shorter period of time, with demonstrably more disciplines, groups and geographies represented. On the other hand, as any first year statistics student will tell you, "data does not equal meaning."

Unfortunately, more participation does not necessarily mean better participation, enhanced learning or increased understanding. The paradoxical effect of more and faster data collection can also, as Jaron Lanier suggests, be less understanding and a greater analytical burden on the practitioner. Whereas past processes may have been slow and cumbersome by today's standards, the difficult process of discovery often allowed time for inductive synthesis and integration of opposing viewpoints, creating meaning even as the trends and drivers are still being uncovered and understood. From a social perspective, many crowdsourcing contributions are essentially one–way, in which the contributor invites the futurist to pay attention to something they have found interesting. Whereas participation in a workshop or scanning exercise often meant engagement in a dialogue, with the potential for pedagogical outcomes, simply adding data to a system through a series of clicks does not offer the same potential.

Participation Problems

Next generation futures systems will therefore have to address the synthesis and interpretation of results in a way that is more substantial and useful than most crowdsourcing solutions today. At the same time, they will also need to engage the social dynamics of participation more directly; why people contribute, what they get out of it, and how it factors into the final product (which will most likely be for a very different, paying, audience).

Noah Raford is an international strategic planner and policy advisor who recently completed a Ph.D. at MIT on how crowdsourcing and the Web are impacting scenario planning.

Many interesting experiments are currently under way that point towards promising opportunities. Yet while it is fairly certain that the use of Web-based participation and content creation in futures work is here to stay, the form it will take is still open. In the meantime, the promise of speed and efficiency gains is likely to produce continued demand for the development of such systems, especially as 'big data' and algorithmic clustering of content becomes more common.

Speeding Up and Dumbing Down

The result will be, at least in the short-term, both a speeding up and a dumbing down of the process, with certain kinds of analytical exercises yielding to the pressures of commodification and automation before others. This can be seen already in the field, where many 'non-futurist' companies provide similar trend tracking and monitoring services, delivered by non-specialists, far more cheaply, with reasonably good results. Similar things have happened right across the service sector, from graphic design to accountancy. Specialists have responded by becoming more adept at more complex projects and more difficult problems. It seems naïve to imagine that futures will somehow escape such a powerful driver of change.

Both Simpler and Richer

If the futures field does follow the same path as other service sectors, we can expect simpler tasks to become quicker, cheaper, and less profitable, while futurists need to demonstrate greater capability to earn the trust of clients. Parts of the product will be less 'original' or 'insightful' by today's handmade standards, but this should free resources for richer analysis of depth and complexity. It is therefore possible that the 'future of futures' may resemble something akin to modern day psychotherapy; anyone will be able to get free (and possibly even accurate) advice from their horoscopes at the back of the newspaper. But professional, personalized service will still come from a cadre of expensive, highly trained, personally trusted advisors; even if the empirical validity of both may still be open to question.

Most Important Futures Works

The Limits to Growth, published in 1972, is based on a computer model which simulated the interaction of biosphere and human activity. The research was commissioned by the Club of Rome. The variables that were modeled were population, industrialization, pollution, food production and resource depletion.

The book was widely criticized after publication – partly on the grounds that it underestimated technology effects. But 40 years on, repeated reviews have found the forecasts from the original model to be strikingly accurate – the most likely outcome being 'overshoot and collapse' during the 2020s. – **Andrew Curry**

INTEGRAL FUTURES

by Richard A. Slaughter

Changing methods and approaches

Futures practice has been dominated by forecasting and scenarios-based approaches. More recently we have seen the emergence of a social construction phase and another described as Integral Futures. Both forecasting and scenarios focus largely on the external world. Critical Futures Studies, on the other hand, examined what might be called the 'social interiors.' That is, it saw the familiar exterior forms of society (populations, technologies, infrastructure and so on) as grounded in, and dependent upon, powerful social factors such as worldviews, paradigms and values.

Futurists had not overlooked the latter, but they were seen as problematic. Methods to incorporate them systematically into futures enquiry and action were needed. Perhaps the central claim of Critical Futures Studies was that it is within these shared symbolic foundations that certain wellsprings of the present lie, as well as the seeds of many possible alternative futures. Since the latter is a guiding concept in futures work generally, locating the origins of these alternatives in the ways that different societies actually worked was a significant step. Critical futures work, however, itself lacked something essential – deeper insight into the nature and dynamics of individual agency. By addressing this missing element Integral Futures has, in a sense, completed a long process of disciplinary development, perhaps resulting in a new phase of innovation and change.

A new map

Some years ago Ken Wilber found a way of integrating the central ideas from a wide variety of disciplines, including scientists, engineers, psychologists and even mystics. His synthesis resulted in a framework that views the world through a four quadrant framework created by a simple division between 'inner' and 'outer' on a vertical axis; and between 'individual' and 'social' on the horizontal one (See Figure overleaf).

Each quadrant records the process of evolution in that domain – from simple stages to more complex ones. Hence there are four parallel processes, each intimately linked with the other: interior-individual development; exterior-individual development; interior-social development and exterior-social development. According to Wilber, "the upper half of the diagram represents individual realities; the lower half, social or communal realities. The right half represents exterior forms – what things look like from the outside; and the left hand represents interior forms – what things look like from within."

The four quadrant model can be further elaborated but even simple versions help us to question the widespread habit of viewing the

> If we focus our attention on the external aspects of our predicament, the global context becomes a trap for humanity.

world as if it were a singular entity – which is how it tends to appear. We unconsciously run quite different domains together, creating endless confusion. Now we can start to see how different principles and tests of truth apply in different domains. This, in turn, brings greater clarity to the kinds of tasks that futurists undertake, as well as opening out more innovative solutions.

Dr. Richard A. Slaughter is a writer, practitioner and innovator in futures studies and applied foresight. His latest book is To See With Fresh Eyes – Integral Futures and the Global Emergency *(2012) Brisbane, Foresight International.*

Figure
The four Integral quadrants.
(Source: Ken Wilber)

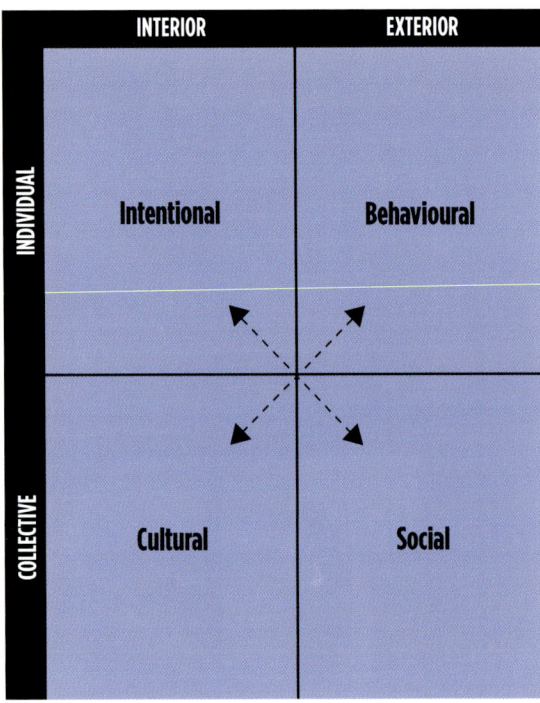

The consequences include:

- a balancing of inner and outer perspectives;
- multiple and yet systematic views of our species' history and development;
- access to the dynamics of social construction, innovation and 'deep design';
- aspects of the 'deep structures' of more advanced civilizations;
- a new focus on the detailed development of the practitioner (not merely his or her cognitive ability); and
- new methods, tools and approaches.

Like any other toolkit or innovation, these tools and perspectives have limitations. Yet even at this relatively early stage they provide new starting points for depth insight, practical wisdom and a more durable foundation for ground-breaking futures work. Part of this involves the shift from conventional to post-conventional stages.

CONSEQUENCES

If we direct our attention mainly to the external aspects of the human predicament then ways forward will forever elude us. The global context becomes a trap for humanity. In practice such conventional 'exterior' approaches to world issues cover only part of the territory. If we also explore the 'interior collective' (society) and the 'interior individual' (the unique world of each person) then it is evident that integral approaches bring new dimensions to futures studies.

CONVENTIONAL TO POST-CONVENTIONAL

Conventional work in any field plays a vital part in the overall picture. It operates within pre-defined boundaries according to defined rules using well-known ideas and methods. A great deal of futures work in the world is like this. It serves well-known needs and clients. It operates in familiar territory: corporations, planning departments, consultancies, government agencies and the like. Those working in this mode tend to focus on the 'exterior collective' domain (technology, the infrastructure, the physical world). Such work can be enhanced by considering post-conventional approaches and explicitly including the interior domains.

Post-conventional work recognizes that the entire external world is constantly 'held together' by interior structures of meaning and value. Two brief examples: the dogged pursuit of economic growth, and viewing nature merely as a set of

---

The entire external world is constantly 'held together' by interior structures of meaning and value.

---

resources for human use. In a post-conventional view, objective accounts of the world are not possible (even within the so-called 'hard' sciences). Rather, human activities everywhere are supported by subtle but powerful networks of value, meaning and purpose that are socially created and often maintained over long periods of time. Post-conventional work draws on these more intangible domains and certainly demands more of practitioners. It means, for example, that a focus on various 'ways of knowing' (e.g. empirical, psychological, critical) becomes unavoidable. Yet the effort involved is certainly worthwhile. Careful and appropriate use of the new methods means that practitioners can gain deeper knowledge and more profound insight into both the currently changing social order as well as its possible futures.

A RICHER VIEW OF HUMAN AGENCY

The next step was to begin to correlate different approaches and methods in futures/foresight work with a new appreciation of the 'individual interiors,' the unique inner world of each person. One widely known approach was through 'spiral dynamics,' based on the work of Clare Graves. It depicted a nested series of 'human operating systems' that provide clues as to what is going on 'under the surface.' The approach can be used as a guide to individual and social interiors but it is not immune to critique and is by no means the only option. Various stage development theorists provide detailed insights into over twenty distinct 'lines of development' in human beings (e.g. values, communication, self concept etc). The practical consequence is that we can gain greater clarity about our own 'ways of knowing', our preferences, strengths, blind spots etc, as well as those of others.

Such developments imply that successful practice involves more than mastering some of the better-known futures techniques. One of the most striking discoveries is that it is levels of development within the practitioner that, more than anything else, determine how well (or badly) any particular methodology will be used or any practical task will be performed. In one sense this is obvious. An inexperienced or poorly trained practitioner will always get inferior results when compared with others who have in-depth personal and professional knowledge. Yet, on the other hand, there are all-too-few professional training programs that take the interior development of practitioners seriously. The experience gleaned at the Australian Foresight Institute and its later iterations provide tangible evidence that support this view.

It is now obvious why the earlier tendency to focus on a practitioner's cognitive development and methodological skills provided an incomplete picture. As Peter Hayward and others have demonstrated, to be a success in any field demands a good deal more than cognitive ability and technical competence. For example, ethical, communicative and interpersonal lines of development are equally vital to the well rounded practitioner.

INTEGRAL FUTURES PRACTICE AND 'PROTO-SOLUTIONS'

Integral Futures frameworks acknowledge the complexity of systems, contexts and interconnected webs of awareness and activity. These all influence the behavior of individuals and groups. They also shape structures and

Interior Human Development
Human developmental factors that frame perception and condition motivation and capacity have primary role. Options for translation and transformation. Re-focuses debate and strategies, on fundamental issues and opens up basis to resolve them.

Exterior Actions
Focuses on what people actually do: their habits, behaviors, and strategies, including strategies of avoidance and the efforts they put in to 'make a difference'. Behavioral drivers and inhibitors. The many applications of design.

Interior Cultural Development
The role of cultures, ideologies, worldviews and language that mediate self and other. Embody socialization frameworks with embedded presuppositions and hierarchies of values. Establishes foundations of economy. Actively selects specific options from much wider range of possibilities

Global system, infrastructure
The physical environment, its cycles of matter and energy. The types of infrastructure(s) superimposed upon it. The kinds of technologies that are employed and their impacts (resource depletion, pollution, ecological simplification, etc.) on the global system. Visible consequences of value, cultural, and design choices.

Figure
Generic 'proto-solutions' to global dilemmas. (Source: R. Slaughter, The Biggest Wake up Call in History, Foresight International, 2010.)

An earlier version of this paper was published as "Integral futures: a new era for futures practitioners", in C. Wagner, Foresight, Innovation and Strategy, Towards a Wiser Future, World Future Society, 2005.

events in the physical, social and psychological worlds. These frameworks incorporate developmental perspectives that recognize individual and collective access to different structures of consciousness, from which a great deal flows. Human development is seen as multi-dimensional, following inter-related, discoverable forms. There are specific ways of understanding and working with different dimensions of development, including how these interact.

In this view innovative problem solving actively acknowledges phenomena from each of the quadrants. They include: the specific ways that stakeholders construct meaning and significance; culturally derived perspectives, rules and systems of meaning; the social infrastructure, including people's concrete skills, behaviors and actions; and, finally, the nature and dynamics of the relevant societal structures and systems. It follows that Integral Futures practitioners will therefore not be content with merely tracking external 'signals

> **Integral Futures practitioners will explore different perspectives to find appropriate approaches in different situations. They'll be open to many perspectives and interpretations.**

of change.' They will also become proficient in exploring different perspectives to find approaches that are appropriate to different situations. They will be open to a wide range of perspectives and interpretations. It is then but a short step to considering the implications of what I refer to as 'proto-solutions' to global dilemmas that emerge from each of the quadrants (See Figure on previous page). I have developed this concept further in my book, *The Biggest Wake-Up Call in History*.

Conclusion

I have argued that Integral approaches to futures enquiry and action provide us with richer options than hitherto. They help us to engage in depth with the multiple crises that threaten our world and its nascent futures. As futurists and foresight practitioners we can look more deeply into ourselves and into our social contexts to find the 'levers of change,' the strategies, the enabling contexts, the pathways to social foresight.

Such work reaches across previously separate realms. It regards exterior developments with the 'eye' of perception that it consciously adopts. It participates in shared social processes and takes careful note of shared objective realities. In other words this is an invitation to move and act in a deeper, richer and more subtly interconnected world. Post-conventional and integrally informed

---

Most Important Futures Works

Six pillars: futures thinking for transforming by Sohail Inayatullah

"Six pillars" is an ambitious attempt to rethink the futures process, compressed into a journal article. Inayatullah, who also developed Causal Layered Analysis, proposes connections between six foundational futures concepts, six questions, and six pillars of practice. The article, published in *Foresight*, also outlines ways to integrate a number of well-known futures techniques, including macro-history, scenarios, futures wheels, integral futures, and emerging issues analysis. Some of the futures history is a little unreliable; the discussion of 'used,' 'disowned,' and 'alternate' futures is particularly rich.
- **Andrew Curry**

futures work is not for the faint-hearted. Yet it suggests a range of constructive responses to a world currently desperate for solutions to the encroaching global emergency.

For more details, including extracts and info on related works, please go to: www.foresightinternational.com.au/.

Further Reading

Beck, Don and Chris Cowan (1996), *Spiral Dynamics*, Blackwell, Malden, Mass.

Collins, Terry and Andy Hines, "The evolution of integral futures – a status update," *World Future Review*, Vol 2, No 3, June-July, 2010, World Future Society, Bethesda MD. Easily the best overview of the development of Integral Futures.

Hayward, Peter, "Resolving the moral impediments to foresight action," *Foresight* 5, 1, 2003.

Ogilvy, Jay, "Futures studies and the human sciences: the case for normative scenarios," in R. Slaughter, (ed) (1996), *New Thinking for a New Millennium*, Routledge, London.

Slaughter, Richard, "A new framework for environmental scanning," *Foresight*, Vol 1, No 5, 1999.

Slaughter, Richard, "Road testing a new model at the Australian Foresight Institute," *Futures*, 36, 2004. Also P. Hayward and J. Voros, "Foresight education in Australia – time for a hybrid model?" *Futures* 43, 2, 2012. Both available at: *http://integralfutures.com/wordpress/?page_id=121*.

Slaughter, Richard (2004), "Changing Methods and Approaches in Futures Studies," in *Futures Beyond Dystopia: Creating Social Foresight*, Routledge, London.

Slaughter, Richard (ed), Integral Futures, *Futures Special issue*, vol 40, No 2, 2008.

Slaughter, Richard (2010), *The Biggest Wake-Up Call in History*, Brisbane, Foresight International.

Slaughter, Richard (forthcoming, 2012), *To See With Fresh Eyes – Integral Futures and the Global Emergency*, Foresight International, Brisbane. For more info see: *http://integralfutures.com/wordpress/?page_id=15*.

Wilber, Ken (1995), *Sex, Ecology, Spirituality: the Spirit of Evolution*, Shambhala, Boston.

Wilber, Ken, (2000), *A Theory of Everything*, Shambhala, Boston.

Wilber, Ken (2000), *Integral Psychology*, Shambhala, Boston.

THE FUTURE OF HUMAN HEALTH TREATMENTS

by Darko Iovrik

In the future, most health treatments will focus on the treatment of chronic diseases, partly motivated by the increasing proportion of the older population, and partly by the desire for eternal life. These approaches will use biotechnology, mainly genetics, in order to achieve increasingly impressive results. The increasing costs and risks of these technologies will require an appropriate government response which might or might not be adequate, leading to the first key uncertainty: the extent and success of regulation in controlling the risks and maximizing the benefits for the wider population. The second uncertainty relates to the clash between two competing visions for humanity: naturally healthy on the one hand, trans-humanist on the other, emphasizing self-development through technology. The latter uncertainty will not be resolved by 2025, but the trend will be clear.

This is a summary of Darko Iovric's paper, which won first place in the Individual Category in the APF's Student Recognition Program in 2009.

FROM VALUES TO TIME

by Marcus Barber

Marcus Barber is the Director of Looking Up Feeling Good Pty Ltd, and a leading strategic futurist in Australia.

Notions of time are central to futures work. By bringing to the fore awareness of variations in people's concepts of time, and therefore of their attitudes to the future, foresight practitioners can more effectively utilize the array of methodologies at their disposal. The Value Systems framework identified by Clare Graves, and later developed by Don Beck and Chris Cowan, provides clues for futurists as to how people understand time differently.

It tends to be approached in three distinct streams – Spiral, Circular and Linear. Where time has a defined start and end (birth then death) the interpretation is of linear progression. Where time is said to have cyclical stages of growth then decay, followed by growth, and so on, it has a Circular nature. When time is interpreted as being a spiral, life and death are intertwined in an upward and continuous evolution – in your next life you take steps towards being more 'complete' as a 'being', with death merely an opportunity to reflect on your progress to date.

Perhaps surprisingly, the most significant benefit in practice from incorporating Value Systems (VS) into foresight work is that it maintains an appreciation for the 'people' element often lost in the trends, forecasting and technology focus of much futures thinking. There are risks too. It is probable that applying

> By bringing to the fore awareness of variations in people's concepts of time, foresight practitioners can more effectively utilize the array of methodologies at their disposal.

Value Systems will expose structural limitations within popular foresight methodologies, and require practitioners to think more deeply about their tools and processes.

VALUE SYSTEMS SUMMARIZED

Value Systems research now extends over 40 years. Graves said his model was "An emergent, cyclical, bio/psycho/social double helix model of adult human behavior." Whilst complex, it accurately describes his theory which suggests adult behavior is influenced by external life conditions and coping abilities of increasing complexity. An individual's approach to dealing with external complexity is influenced by their biological and psychological makeup. These two inter-related streams provided Graves with a double helix linkage. More complex thinking in dealing with life conditions provided his 'emergent' stages, swinging between 'self orientation' and 'others' orientation, providing the cyclical nature of development.

Cowan and Beck added a shorthand for the model in the form of color codes. Their intention was to make Graves' complex VS notational style more accessible. Their color codes have led to a wide level of discussion in a number of communities of practice which have begun to interpret the research data. For this article, it is worth noting that all of Graves' research confirmed that there are differing approaches to how people cope with their external environments. These differing approaches create the variations in how people deal with the concept of the future.

In any of these contexts of time, it is usually the future that draws us forward. In this sense, 'things that happened' (past), 'things that are happening' (present) and 'things that might happen' (future) enable people to interpret or classify their understanding of events in time. Each Value System has its own interpretation of past, present and future, yet these differences are commonly ignored in futures work.

> When our thinking is shallow or misinformed, we increase the possibility of being surprised by unanticipated events.

A 'western worldview' is a singular group, as is an 'economic worldview' or 'technological worldview.' In taking a singular approach, futurists ignore distinct interpretations viewed through the eyes of differing Value Systems. What passes for 'technology' to one group can be very different to another. What counts as an appropriate model of inclusiveness to one VS is unlikely to be the same for another. This is a process-orientated dimension, in much the same way that thinking about time is a process. Essentially this approach asks us to deal more with the 'how' than the 'what' (often referred to as 'content').

The implications for the way in which foresight methodologies are applied are significant. Selecting the 'right' tool requires the foresight practitioner to consider how the particular method is applied or fits each of the thinking processes, or Value System.

Strategic Foresight Awareness in Value Systems

For the most part, foresight operates at an unconscious level. When our expectations are unrealistic and our thinking shallow or misinformed, we increase the possibility of being surprised by unanticipated events. This is why we hear constantly of people who are shocked when a foreseeable event occurs (a stock market crash, a collision on a busy street).

Value Systems expand our concepts of strategic foresight by alerting us to variables in approaches to the future. To learn from our 'mistakes of judgment and anticipation' we need to be able to assess 'how' we came to develop our beliefs, and seek to improve next time. This understanding provides a framework through which we can see what data will be first filtered by each Value System, prior to it being accepted as relevant and valid. Information that does not fit within an individual's established VS framework will typically be discarded or ignored.

Certain Value Systems are more likely to operate at a strategic level when utilizing foresight; for others, bringing to conscious awareness information not previously considered will succeed only where that information fits within the VS process an individual uses. What is true for individuals is often true of organizations, which raises a whole new futures dynamic. Questions about how a futurist engages with clients or partners, via 'action' and 'inquiry' (see Rooke and Torbert's 1998 model) and notions of 'open' and 'closed' (Rokeach, 1960) are also rich emerging areas for futures practice.

By consciously thinking about the future we begin to create deep, broad and rich strategic foresight approaches. Value Systems help futurists maintain a focus on humanity – arguably the core purpose of much futures thinking.

Further Reading

Beck, Don, and Chris Cowan (1996), *Spiral Dynamics*. Blackwell.

Rokeach, Milton (1960), *The Open and Closed Mind*. Basic Books.

Rooke, David, and William Torbert (1998), "Organizational transformation as a function of CEOs' developmental stage." *Organization Development Journal* 16.

An earlier, and longer, version of this article was published in Futures Research Quarterly Volume 21 Number 2 (Summer 2005). More information on the Value Systems framework can be found at the National Values Centre, http://www.spiraldynamics.com/.

FROM DESIGN FICTION TO EXPERIENTIAL FUTURES

by Noah Raford

Noah Raford is an international strategic planner and policy advisor with a background in architecture and design.

Experiential futures, design fiction, artifacts from the future or speculative fiction. Regardless of its name, there has been a surge in this kind of futures work in the last 24 months. Advocates such as Stuart Candy, Bruce Sterling, Anab Jain, Justin Pickard and Julian Bleecker argue that design-based futures are not just a shiny form of communication, but are a distinct way of practicing futures research itself. Highly visual, often emotional, and ethnographically infused, their approach brings the future alive through videos, objects, and print media. The result, they argue, is a profoundly engaging experience that goes beyond technical reports and PowerPoint presentations towards a different form of engagement.

Of course, 'experiential' and immersive activities have always played an important role in certain kinds of futures work, particularly in the early days of scenario practice at GBN. The very notion of a 'learning journey,' for example, represents just such an immersive, experiential activity. But a new generation of practitioners is tackling some core issues of foresight with a fresh eye, bringing a liberal dose of creativity that is both powerful and engaging. Straddling the worlds of visual media, theater, film making, industrial design, and management consulting, design futures may be coming into its own as a distinct sub-discipline.

There are important differences between experiential futures, design futures, and speculative fiction (see the Figure on the facing page for a mapping of related terms by Justin Pickard), but for the purposes of this essay, I would like instead to emphasize their similarities. Most design futures strive to create a rich, textured, often first person immersion in a credible alternate world through the use of multiple media and storytelling techniques. The best examples also seek to evoke the everyday richness of life in a 'thick' way, going beyond the obvious layers to explore more subtle 'scents and sounds' of an alternative future in more emotional, evocative ways. In doing so, design futures uses the familiar and everyday to help achieve the futurist's goal of "making the familiar strange and the strange, familiar" (in the words of Stewart Brand). The attention to detail in many such projects, whether physical, visual or textual, helps to immerse the viewer in a direct narrative relationship with the material. This can produce profound insight into the kinds of products, services and stakeholders who may inhabit this scenario.

These approaches come with certain risks, however. Because they can so powerfully create a compelling, self-contained experience for the viewer, design futures are often at risk of producing visually rich, but analytically impoverished, outputs. Corning, the industrial glass manufacturer responsible for the wildly successful "A Day Made of Glass" videos, is a case in point. Although it is a beautifully made video and a masterpiece of public relations, critics point out that it lacks the most basic considerations of causal relationships and interactive effects. As a piece of film-making, it is engaging. As a piece of scenarios work, however, it falls below the mark.

While many argue that it is not Corning's job to produce rigorous scenarios of the future (and they are right), this example illustrates how easy it can be to produce a visually rich design that is 'all sizzle and no sausage.' It is therefore of particular importance for practicing futurists to

Figure 1 – Mapping Design and Experiential Futures Terrain. (Source: Justin Pickard, "My Radio Prefers Bacon", APF V-Gathering online presentation. 2011)

FORESIGHT
horizon-scanning
science fiction
scenarios
roadmaps   experiential futures   'new journalism'   GONZO
futurescaping   design ethnography
design fiction   culture-jamming
concept art
'critical design'
interaction design
user research
prototyping
DESIGN

GALLERY

SONG OF THE MACHINE (2011), BY SUPERFLUX

http://superflux.in/work/song-machine

"What if we could change our view of the world with the flick of a switch?" This is the question posed by the design futures consultancy, Superflux Studios, based in London. In the short video, "Song of the Machine," it tracks the everyday life of a single person as he goes about his business; totally blind, were it not for the help of a retinal prostheses which can see infrared, ultraviolet and visible spectrums.

Image from Song of the Machine courtesy of Superflux

use these approaches in combination with other forms of research and analysis. Even better, practicing futurists should work closely with new entrants to the field to help improve everyone's practice. Such a synthesis would reinvigorate futures practice while bringing new rigor and insight to the design process.

Experiential futures is a powerful addition to the foresight toolbox. It is doubly important because many of its leading practitioners are from outside the self-defined futures community. They include artists, designers, science fiction authors, video game creators and film-makers. The varied interests and agendas of these groups suggests that design futures will be an important source of continued inspiration, negotiation and creative tension for the foresight community in the coming years. While it may not be a generational shift of Kuhnian proportion, it does represent a turn in futures work that is both vital and important to the future of the field. It is for this reason that we present here a selection of interesting design futures work.

36

Image of Fly Me To The Moon courtesy of Purple Tornado

Funded by Science Dublin and with help from optogenetic scientists, the video is powerful precisely because it is so quotidian. One young man's day is followed in intimate detail – riding on the train, meeting a friend – but augmented with a fantastic technology rendered normal through every day use.

"Song of The Machine' takes real-world science and imaginatively pushes it to its limits. [It's] a great example of how science and engineering illuminate what's possible while design helps zero in on what's preferable."
– John Pavlus, Co.Design, June 2011

FLY ME TO THE MOON (2011), BY PURPLE TORNADO
http://www.youtube.com/watch?v=pbZu1WNJNLQ

"Fly Me to the Moon" is a short video developed by APF member Heather Schlegel for the financial transaction company, SWIFT. On the surface, it explores the future for electronic payments. Beyond that, it explores how concepts of trust, identity, ease, convenience and technology will interact with money in the future. It is told with realistic characters, emotion and social meaning, embedded in an everyday world of remarkable richness and depth.

Four friends sit around a restaurant table, chatting about old stories. One, a pilot, discusses how much fun it is flying into space for her job. The friends discuss space tourism with the kind of casual amazement that one might experience backstage at a concert. It is amazing, but not earth shattering. Why? Because like all things, it has already become part of the fabric of everyday life.

This project is subtle and compelling. Like the best kinds of design future hybrids, it is also well researched and rich with strategic insight. It works both as an excellent piece of futures research and as an engaging piece of media and entertainment. Even more interesting, it manages to do so with practically no special effects or high technology.

ADAMS & SMITH (2009), BY HOLLINGTON AND KYPRIANOU
http://www.electronicsunset.org/node/1579

Ethnographic design futurist Scott Smith suggests that one of the most compelling aspects of design fiction is the use of physical objects as entry points into a conversation about the future (as opposed to just the end-product).

"Adams & Smith," from artists Hollington & Kyprianou, does just this. A fictitious auction house, Adams & Smith (founded in 2034) hosts an auction in the year 2059 of early 21st century collectable products. It includes a gallery exhibit of the objects, a printed and online catalogue, and a live auction event with theatrics, staging and full production.

The items for auction include the Double Buggy Perambulator, which is "a wonderful reminder of the folly of unrestricted growth of the human population before the Last Depression." A pack of cigarettes is included with the curatorial observation that, "one of the most interesting aspects of late capitalist culture – and one that should be remembered whenever comrades may feel our current struggles and problems overwhelming – was the self destructive nature of so many of the desperate people who had the misfortune of populating it."

Lot Number 8, a "genuine example of late capitalist water contained in an original,

Image of Auction of the Future courtesy of Hollington and Kyprianou

scientifically-verified as sealed plastic container," is included as an example of the commodification of public goods, while a box of pain-killers prompts the reflection that, "one of the many curiosities of the late capitalist period was the way in which populations were controlled via medication and health policies."

The project creates a fictional world where a hyper-consumerist capitalism has eaten itself, giving way to an anarcho-communalist resilient economy. "Each lot reveals a curious aspect of that bygone age, shedding light on the odd and dangerously contradictory practices of the time," they write, disrupting our experience of our present.

Although not a 'futures' project, it is an excellent demonstration of how everyday objects can be used to spark a conversation about what may seem absurd or unthinkable in the past, or in the future.

ARK-INC (2008), by Superflux
http://superflux.in/work/ark-inc

"Despite repeated warnings that we are fast approaching a point of no return, the world's governments (and ourselves) pay these issues little more than lip service."

ARK-INC is a fictional company and set of products created by designer Jon Ardern (also of Superflux). The company "offers products and services as investments in the creation of a 'post-crash' portfolio that will hold or gain value as the world of traditional economics crumbles."

As well as a compelling, post-disaster shop front which customers can visit, ARK-INC developed a series of 'Second Life' products, such as the ARK RADIO, a high design radio that would look at home on any stylish, contemporary table. After the collapse, however, the product can be converted to run on solar power and operate as an encrypted two-way audio and data transmission device, thereby creating a self-powered communications network.

The products, publication, installation, website and accompanying videos demonstrate the power of cross-platform 'transmedia' approaches. It was so convincing, in fact, that despite clear notices on the website, Ardern continues to receive inquiries by concerned collapsitarians seeking to buy his devices.

Calling such an approach "superfiction," ARK-INC demonstrates yet other way that design can be used to create both compelling visions of tomorrow, and powerful lenses to re-interpret today.

Image of ARK-INC courtesy of Superflux

Image of Our Plastic Century courtesy of Jake Dunagan.

OUR PLASTIC CENTURY (2010), by Candy, Kornfeld, Dunagan, and Nichols
http://www.iftf.org/node/3507

"Shallow are the souls that have forgotten how to shudder." – Leon Kass.

In their project "Our Plastic Century" a team of designers including futurists Stuart Candy and Jake Dunagan (both APF members) sought to create an installation that would trigger "the wisdom of repugnance." It was an attempt to visualize and extrapolate trends in ocean pollution that debuted at the California Academy of Sciences in 2010.

The Plastic Century project used four large water coolers filled with plastic debris to represent the total amount of plastic in Earth's oceans at different points in time: the birth of Jacques Cousteau (1910); 1960; the present; and forecast out to 2030. Viewers were invited literally to drink from each water container, an invitation that produced severe reactions of disgust in some participants.

"Our goals for the project were three-fold," Dunagan explained in the project's blog post. "First, we wanted to show, in a compelling way, the exponential growth of plastic production over the last 100 years, and project the levels into the future if no interventions are taken. Second, we wanted to demonstrate that water, pollution, and humans are intimately connected; plastic doesn't go 'away.' And third, we sought to trigger the 'wisdom of repugnance' and install a level of disgust that will stick with people beyond the initial experience."

The project used a visual and intuitive approach, provoking powerful reactions. Its projection of plastic accumulation evoked the futurist's goal of "making the familiar strange and the strange, familiar."

"We are trying to recalibrate people's reality," wrote Dunagan. The installation transports the viewer into a future world, grabs them emotionally, and then suggests new ways of seeing their behavior today. It is a powerful example of using installations to evoke emotional dialogues about future issues.

ANTICIPATION: THE DISCIPLINE OF UNCERTAINTY

by Riel Miller

Futurists are haunted by an unresolved problem – how to deal with the unknowable and novelty rich future. Most futurists in the APF and elsewhere have accepted for some years now that prediction and probability are limited ways of thinking about the future. But knowing what does not work is not the same as knowing what does. The paradox of futures is that we can't find ways to 'know' the future, but rather we need to find ways to live and act with not-knowing the future. This requires the discipline of anticipation (DOA).

What is Disciplinarity?

Discipline is by definition an encounter with constraints. In this sense the development and description of a discipline, be it the mastery of a stonemason or the expertise of an economics professor, is based on how practice confronts and works within the limits imposed by the discipline. Once a discipline is well established, the terms and institutions that define and limit the practice become familiar and obvious. For instance, in the mid-twentieth century economics as a university-based discipline was consistently defined in introductory textbooks (such as Samuelson) as the study of the "allocation of scarce resources amongst competing ends." Such formulations, as well as the systems that reproduce and alter disciplinary knowledge, evolve over time. This short essay is not meant to offer a comprehensive analysis of the theory and practice, debates and experience, power and history that give rise to and reshape the contours of a discipline. Rather, considering the contributions of the APF and the experiences of futurists around the world, the focus is on the need for disciplinarity and an initial sketch of what such a discipline entails.

Why Disciplinarity?

The motivating hypothesis of this piece is that the time has come for futurists to collaborate to develop a discipline concerned with the nature, role and use of the future, both in human systems and more generally as part of our efforts to understand our anticipatory universe. There is a number of reasons, summarized briefly here, that justify an effort by futurists to elaborate a discipline:

- Philosophy and science have opened up new ways of defining the universe and understanding what is the future.
- Due to specific attributes of the present, success in using the future without a discipline is reaching its limits – both in terms of the quality of the processes and outcomes.
- Values and tools, aspirations and daily practices are generating the potential to use the future differently, but this potential cannot be grasped without the assurance – depth of knowledge, trustworthiness, legitimacy, visibility – afforded by disciplinarity.
- The emergence of a discipline of anticipation, focused on defining and using the future more effectively, is already underway. By making an explicit commitment to this project futurists can both enhance the speed and quality of the work.

A discipline offers at least three advantages:
1. **Depth:** that by circumscribing what is legitimately included within the claims of knowing, a discipline can focus on developing an expertise (specialization), deepening its theory and practice;
2. **Identity:** through such specialization, and the specialized language that goes with it, both the practitioner (from apprentice to master) and the outsider (layperson) can identify the

Dr. Riel Miller is one of the world's leading strategic foresight designers and practitioners. He has recently been appointed Head of Foresight at UNESCO in Paris. For further details see: www.rielmiller.com.

discipline as concerned with a specific subject matter and why it is trustworthy;

3. **Legitimacy:** depth and identity help to foster responsibility and legitimacy – the foundations (but not a guarantee) of trustworthiness and motivation for investing in the stocks/flows of a discipline (which include reputational assets and attention to excellence).

The Discipline of Anticipation (DOA)

When framed as a discipline, 'anticipation' entails the acquisition and use of a set of design principles for thinking about the 'later-than-now.' When someone becomes more capable at anticipation they become better at using the future to understand the present. They are more capable because they are better able to do three general tasks. They can (1) clarify the specific purposes of thinking about the future; (2) establish a consistent relationship between the aims of futures thinking and the methods used to do so; and (3) achieve greater sophistication, as is to be expected when disciplinarity brings greater depth, clarity and legitimacy. These are accepted attributes of mastery acquired through learning.

My initial propositions for general design principles for the Discipline of Anticipation (DOA) fall into four categories:

1. A descriptive proposition that defines what is the future.
2. A sensemaking proposition that calls for an anticipatory systems point-of-view for the discipline as a whole.
3. A taxonomic proposition that distinguishes the three distinct but practically overlapping forms that conscious anticipation can take in the present.
4. An organizational proposition that offers rules for conducting and organizing anticipatory processes according to the principles of the scientific method (hypothesis testing and external review).

The Discipline of Anticipation – An Initial Specification

1. **The future defined.** The DOA assumes that the future is defined by four fundamental attributes of our universe: the practical irreversibility of time; birth and death – difference and repetition; unforeseeable novelty; and connectedness.

    i. Time is irreversible and continuous/contiguous. 'Time travel' cannot be done. Despite the multi-dimensionality of time/space there is no way to leap from the present into the past or future. So, in practical terms, the future does not exist outside of the present. The future is a presently imagined 'later in time.'

The Components of the Future

"I believe it is useful to assume that 'the future' will derive from three components. One will be the continuation of things found in the present, and also found in the past

The second component will be things that existed in the past, but not in the present, that will appear again in the future – and their opposite: things that did not exist in the past but are very much a part of the present but that will not exist (or be as important) in the future. These things often appear as cycles or 'spirals'.

The third component will be novelties – things that do not exist now and never existed before, but will in the future."

- James Dator,
Alternative Futures for KWaves

*Source:
http://www.futures.hawaii.edu/publications.html*

ii. Birth and death, difference and repetition. In our universe new entities and entities of entities (assemblages) can come into existence, emerge in the present, be born and can also disappear or die. Without this basic premise dynamics or change cannot exist and the 'later than now' would just be the same as 'now'. Continuity also occurs, as what is now is then repeated in the after. This gives rise to a number of categories of the future in the present, including 'latency' which is the potential of phenomena to become and to repeat, manifesting emergence and inertia over time.

iii. Unforeseeable novelty, the determinants of which do not fully exist in the present, means that the present only partially determines what happens 'later than now.' Novelty, something from nothing, emerges in ways that can fundamentally alter the present. Even if we had perfect knowledge of all aspects of the present, and perfect models of how all aspects of the present interact, the emergent present would still contain surprises. This means we live with creative causality as well as continuity causality.

iv. Connectedness takes many forms, but what it means for the 'later than now' is that there are connections and interactions that span time, acting across different levels of reality. As a result we live in a universe where there can be inertia and rupture, continuity and transformation as well as inter-dependence. This means that the future (i.e., what we imagine in the present) can be about preservation, destruction, and the capacity to perceive and act on emergence.

Anticipation is an attribute of the present that is embedded in physical and social phenomena as they emerge.

Planted on this foundation the Discipline of Anticipation can offer practical ways to describe, locate and track change in its many guises, while consistently and effectively understanding that the 'later than now' is always imaginary.

2. **Anticipatory systems.** Anticipation is a 'real' attribute of the present, embedded within the functioning of physical and social phenomena as they re-emerge and emerge into the present. The anticipatory systems perspective explicitly seeks to take into account the full range of inanimate and animate anticipation. This is critical for disciplinarity because it sets the general framework for trying to understand and use the vast range of specific forms of anticipation – forms that are also context specific. Taking an anticipatory systems perspective assists the discipline to make distinctions across forms and context, linking tasks and tools according to consistent principles and observations.

3. **Categories of the potential of the present.** Categorization of different 'kinds' of anticipation, distinct definitions of what is the future in the present ('being without existing'), facilitate the practical task of imagining the future. The three types of future that exist in the present, and need to be distinguished by futurists in order to enhance the sophistication of anticipation, are:
(1) contingent futures that can be imagined as the outcome of external forces;
(2) optimization futures that assume systemic continuity and implicitly or explicitly 'colonize' the future by assuming that specific outcomes will pertain; and
(3) novel futures that have no imminent cause but spring into existence, altering the present. Of course, all three categories interact and are inter-dependent. These categories are particularly helpful in applied anticipation, taken up in the next principle.

The Creative Mind

In *The Creative Mind* (1911), Henri Bergson argued for turning on its head the common sense view that possibilities precede actual choices. He argued that it is experience that precedes possibility and that we 'see' the options in the past once we know the present.

The following thought experiment helps to illustrate this hypothesis: Imagine you come to a fork in the road without knowing which one to take to reach your destination. You turn left and discover it is the wrong direction. It is then – at that moment, constructed in the reflexivity of our actions and inter-actions, that you know that you made a mistake. Only now, the possibility of turning right exists in the past.

Novelty can be understood in a similar way, it inspires the identification of possibilities in the past. These are possibilities that could not be known in the present because the future of complex realities is unknowable. Such possibilities arise not because of ignorance (something that could potentially be known) but because creative novelty happens and changes what we know and reflexively construct in the present, including possibilities in the past.

4. **The practice of the DOA as a capacity.** Since the Discipline of Anticipation is a way to use the future to learn (creating knowledge) it is therefore a form of research or cognitive engagement/construction. Consequently the DOA as practice consists of activities that always involve narrative (sense making), collective intelligence, and framing/reframing. This is a scientific meta-framework for sensing and making sense of the present that ensures that the way we use the imaginary future is consistent with the three preceding principles.

Each of these premises is necessary, and all are inter-dependent. Taken together, these are design principles for using the future. Or, to put it in different terms, building a more complete and rigorous connection between the definition of what is the future, as emergent, rich, and unknowable novelty, and how to gain an understanding of the imagined future, through the narratives we invent in the present, calls for a set of design principles that take into account the four premises of the Discipline of Anticipation.

Of course, the conventional position in much of the futures community is to use a threefold categorization that distinguishes probable, possible and visionary, or preferred, futures. The first is based mostly on models and data that forecast the future probabilistically using the past; the second is rooted in scenarios that tell more or less imaginative stories about different 'possible' futures (often difficult to distinguish from the first category); and the third is a more normative and sometimes imaginative image of hoped-for tomorrows. In practice, though, the predominant response is to seek out lines of probable cause – using trends, drivers and other sources of 'likely' (or unlikely) outcomes – that attempt in one way or another to discover 'how the future might unfold.'

As a result the purpose and methods of anticipatory thinking tend to be dominated by probabilistic analysis. Which, as is generally accepted, must rest one way or another on continuity-type causal explanations. This excludes novelty that cannot be imagined through causality and cannot be identified from within a rigorous probabilistic framework. The search for causal continuity narrows both the definition of the future and the methods for apprehending it.

It is worth noting that the DOA does not constrain how we go about imagining the future. Today's futurists have access to a wide and refined panoply of tools. Professional futurists have an impressive toolkit, ways of undertaking anticipatory thinking that range from Jay Ogilvy's 'scenaric stance' and Sohail Inayatullah's Causal Layered Analysis to the Ken Wilber-inspired Integral Futures and the Global Business Network's four-quadrant scenarios. (The last two are discussed elsewhere in this book). All of these techniques and many more are potentially useful, depending on the context. The point is that disciplinarity can help practitioners to insist on embracing the fundamental unknowability of the future and to include anticipatory methods and goals that are liberated from the reductionist constraints of probability, continuity and the reductionist projection of existing frames into the future.

Conclusion

Few aspects of our conscious reality are as powerful as the imagined future for determining what we do. For organizations like governments and firms, and families and communities, the future is often the primary reason for doing (even being). By helping to use the future better, in particular by diversifying the use of the future away from heretofore dominant methods – such as probability and planning – and embracing the ambiguity of creative novelty, the development and diffusion of the Discipline of Anticipation can change what people and organizations do. It offers one way to reconcile the way we use the future with the aspirations we have for our capacity to be free. There is no way to know if this will be 'better' or 'worse,' there is no way to know what will happen, but at least human hubris may be tempered by the exigencies of a discipline that seeks to enjoy the amazing creativity of our universe.

With thanks to my colleagues in the APF, the FuMee group, and the editor of this volume, Andrew Curry.

Further reading

Curry, Andrew and Wendy Schultz, (2009), "Roads Less Travelled: Different Methods, Different Futures," *Journal of Future Studies*, May, Vol. 13, No. 4.

Fuller, Ted and Krista Loogma, (2009), "Constructing Futures: A Social Constructivist perspective on foresight methodology," *Futures*, Vol. 41, Issue 2.

FuMee 3, "Unfolding the Present, Spontaneity and Mercury's Arrow," http://fumee.co.cc/?page_id=7.

Mermet, Laurent, Ted Fuller and Rudd van der Helm, (2009), "Re-examining and renewing theoretical underpinnings of the Futures field: A pressing and long-term challenge," *Futures*, Vol. 41, Issue 2.

Mermet, Laurent, (2009) "Extending the perimeter of reflexive debate on futures research: An open framework," *Futures*, Vol. 41, Issue 2.

Miller, Riel, (2011), "Being Without Existing: The Futures Community at a Turning Point? A Comment on Jay Ogilvy's Facing the Fold," *Foresight*, Vol. 13, No. 3.

Miller, Riel and Roberto Poli, (2010), "Anticipatory Systems and the Philosophical Foundations of Futures Studies," *Foresight*, Vol. 12, Issue 3.

Poli, Roberto, (2010), "An Introduction to the Ontology of Anticipation," *Futures*, Vol. 42, Issue 7.

Rossel, Pierre, (2010), "Making Anticipatory Systems More Robust," *Foresight*, Vol. 12, Issue 3.

Tuomi, Ilkka, (forthcoming), "Foresight in an Unpredictable World," *Technology Analysis and Strategic Management*.

THE FUTURE IS A VERB NOT A NOUN

by Tom P. Abeles

Tom P. Abeles is President of Sagacity, Inc, and editor of the journal On The Horizon.

Jesus verbo no sustantivo – Ricardo Arjona

Futures has dwelt in the arena of the pragmatic, of practice, focusing on the needs of clients. But while it has struggled to legitimize itself as a practice, it still dreams of becoming an academic discipline, a dream deferred by its lack of a strong ontological and epistemological frame. This problematic goes all the way back to the 17th and 18th centuries, when the early social scientists believed their studies could yield to the techniques that had proven so successful in the natural and physical sciences.

This tension becomes evident in the efforts of Bertrand de Jouvenel in his book *The Art of Conjecture*, where he defines the arenas of *facta* and *futura*. The former deals with measurable 'facts,' the latter exists more in the domain of conjecture, the domain of the future, which lacked the epistemological foundation needed to be a science. As Roberto Poli points out in a recent article, Wendell Bell introduced in *Foundations of Future Studies* the term 'dispositions' as a bridge between *facta* and *futura*, and others are working on various epistemological frames. (This issue is discussed by Riel Miller in his essay earlier in this book). Yet a firm ontological and epistemological foundation for futures as a discipline, rather than a practice, remains elusive.

SCIENCE AND DISRUPTION

At the same time, the emergence of complexity science may be creating a sufficient disruption in how science is carried out, changing the epistemological underpinnings of disciplines in both sciences and social studies. In turn this could change the nature of futures and challenge large parts of its existing practice.

Complexity science suggests that typical mathematical models may be unstable within the range being studied, and thus either produce false results or different results each time the models are run. In the world of complexity, it seems, one cannot step into the same river twice. For example, equations are composed of both variables and coefficients. The latter are relational constants. But complexity science suggests that the constants are only constant within a narrow time frame.

The metaphor can be extended. There a possibility both that the map, or defining equation, is changing and that the material on which it is drawn may also be changing. With traditional maps, the surface is normally expected to be planar, continuous and static. For the physical sciences, in the majority of applications, both the surface and the constants defining the relationship between variables are expected to hold, for the most part.

In his forthcoming book, *Culturematic*, Grant McCracken describes a 'Culturematic' as "a little machine for making culture." His model is an evolutionary one, of scores of probes, or thousands, which scale up when they discover the conditions for success. (As importantly, they also fail, early and often.)

This is a version of addressing the uncertainty of the future which is gaining more traction. In his book McCracken suggests that scenarios, strategy projections, and planning are going dark. It is easier to launch small, cheap, probes into the environment of choice and sense the results. In many ways this is similar to Wendell Bell's 'dispositions,' existing between facta and futura, where conditions can condense theory into actuality, crossing the boundaries between the scientific and the social arena.

Similarly, the work of David Snowden at Cognitive Edge suggests that under this emerging paradigm, hindsight does not lead to foresight. The implication is that neither the practice nor the discipline of futures can look towards the past. Ferreting out weak signals or emerging issues may produce a false future since both signal and context are dynamic, with respect both to when (time to the future) and to what (emergent properties).

A New Paradigm

One of the problems with futures is that few in the arena track the work being done in knowledge management, particularly the theories developed by Max Boisot in his seminal work, *Knowledge Assets*. Snowden, who collaborated extensively with Boisot, argues that we are going through a third transformative change. After a science-based paradigm gave way to a systems-based paradigm, a complexity-based paradigm is now emerging. George Land postulated that S-curved transitions such as these are stressful, and so humans tend to want to repeat the previous curves rather than take the risk of leaping to a new paradigm. Snowden focuses on those willing to jump. Land suggests that those who hesitate may die.

The question for futures, as a practice or a discipline, is whether is has the tools to jump to a new world of complexity, or whether it will be trapped in the systems-based paradigm in which it evolved. If it is to be the latter, the future of futures seems bleak.

Further Reading

De Jouvenel, Bertrand (1967), *The Art of Conjecture*. Weidenfeld and Nicholson.

Poli, Roberto (2011), "Steps Toward an Explicit Ontology of the Future," *Journal of Future Studies*, 16(1).

Bell, Wendell (2003), *Foundations of Futures Studies*. Transaction Publishers.

Boisot, Max (1998), *Knowledge Assets*, Oxford University Press. Oxford.

Land, George, *Grow or Die,* Leadership 2000, Inc. (Land has also been known as Lock-Land or Ainsworth-Land and versions of this book have had different publishers. A business-oriented version, *Breakpoint and Beyond* was co-written with Beth Jarmon.)

Boisot, Max and Bill McKelvey (2010), "Integrating Modernist and Postmodernist Perspectives on Organizations," *Academy of Management Review*, 35(3).

McElvey, Bill and Max Boisot (2009), "Redefining Strategic Foresight," in L. Constanza and B. MacKay (eds), *Handbook of Research on Strategy and Foresight*. Edward Elgar Publishing.

THE FUTURES OF LITERACY

by Elizabeth Chapman

Pierre Bourdieu wrote that "[l]anguage is not only an instrument of communication or even of knowledge, but also an instrument of power." In the next decades, that instrument will receive several significant upgrades, to become even more powerful. With it, we will be able to construct and decipher meaning in ways we never thought possible. Yet perhaps the most important lesson is that, just like any other tool, we must wield our new literacy carefully. In a time of great social transformation, there always exists the potential for a society to remake itself into something worse than it was before. Leonard Shlain ties the great religious wars and witch hunts of Europe directly to the invention of the printing press, which spread superstitious propaganda; he attributes the rise of the Nazis in Germany to the widespread use of the radio, which allowed Hitler's speeches into every home in the country. Perhaps the ability to think critically will be the most important skill a person from 2060 ought to have to be literate.

Extracted from Elizabeth Chapman's winning entry in the individual category in the APF Student Recognition program in 2010.

AFTERWORD: THE FUTURE OF FUTURES

by Andrew Curry

The notion of futures as a separate practice is now around 50-60 years old. In dating it in this way, I am placing the origins somewhere between Fred Polak's book *The Image of the Future*, Gaston Berger's founding of the Centre International de Prospective, and the creation of the Hudson Institute in 1961 by Herman Kahn as the first bespoke futures consultancy.

Much of the futures practice we have now would be recognizable to these pioneers, in terms of methods, of practice, even of clients.

So what would a futures practice look like that was more strange to those pioneering practitioners? Or, in the words of Alex Pang in his paper 'Futures 2.0': "If the field of futures were invented today... what would it look like?"

We are starting to see some clues. Looking back at the contributions to this book, here is my assessment of the characteristics which will shape the future of futures.

1. It will be more distributed and more networked, more at home with the social media tools which are starting to pervade other research practices, as Alex Pang observed in answering his own question. It is still early days: we know that networked futures can do some things well, other things less well. There will, though, be more data.

2. Futures will find its own way to make the "complexity turn" (to use John Urry's phrase) which has characterized the intellectual life of almost every discipline in the past 30 years. While the futures academy has already engaged with complex adaptive systems and emergence, these have been slower to inform futures methods.

3. Futures will rediscover some of its roots in philosophy, building (or re-building) a knowledge base that places more emphasis on *how* we know what we say we know when we make claims for futures work. The epistemology and ontology of futures work will become increasingly visible.

4. Different ways of knowing, exemplified by approaches which emphasize the importance of values and of experiential understanding, will become more evident in futures practice.

5. Futures will become better informed about its history and its contexts – leading to practice based on a richer understanding of methods and their rationale.

6. Futures was born into a world of growth, the emerging consumer economy, and the Cold War. It will grow up in an age of 'descent'; futures that address a world of resource shortage or even collapse will no longer be regarded as dystopian. One implication is that we may see a resurgence in visioning as a part of futures practice.

All practices have a context, and the contexts here go beyond those of an emerging discipline finding its feet. Futures practice has been fortunate, perhaps, to reach this stage in its evolution at a time when the North Atlantic financial crisis continues to spread such a large political and economic shadow, and when the politics of energy and resource scarcity are becoming rapidly more visible.

Taken together, these represent an eighty-year crisis, and perhaps even a three-hundred year one. New ways of imagining the world are more urgent than ever. The challenges are huge: never was there a better time to test the implicit claim made by all futurists, that good futures work can make a difference. The evolution towards richer and deeper methods, which allow us to 'disturb the present' in more fundamental ways, could not come at a more necessary time.